Bob Larson

The Seduction of America's Youth

THOMAS NELSON PUBLISHERS
Nashville

Published in Nashville, Tennessee, by Thomas Nelson, Inc. and distributed in Canada by Lawson Falle, Ltd., Cambridge, Ontario.

Interior design by J. S. Laughbaum

Unless otherwise noted, Scripture quotations are from THE NEW KING JAMES VERSION of the Bible. Copyright © 1979, 1980, 1982, Thomas Nelson, Inc., Publishers.

Library of Congress Cataloging-in-Publication Data

Larson, Bob.
    Satanism : the seduction of America's youth / by Bob Larson.
      p. cm.
    Includes bibliographical references.
    ISBN 0-8407-3034-9
    1. Satanism—United States. 2. Teenagers—United States—
—Religious life. I. Title.
BF1548.L37   1989
133.4'22'0973—dc20   89–38105
                                          CIP

Printed in the United States of America
3 4 5 6 7 8 9 10 11 12 13 14 15 16 17 18 19 20 21 22 23 24 25 95 94 93 92 90 89

CONTENTS

Part Five
Everyday Armageddons

Part One

The Devil's Disciples

1

Altar of Sacrifice

"I'll murder for the devil. I'm just waiting."

"Waiting for what?" I asked.

Unfortunately, David's boastful claim wasn't new to me. I'd heard the same swagger from other teenagers involved in Satanism. My immediate response in such instances is to find out if the teenager is just bragging or if he really means it.

"I'm seventeen now. If the devil makes me happy and gives me what I want until I'm nineteen, I'll kill as many people as he wants after that. I'll keep on doing it until I'm killed."

David called my radio talk show, "TALK-BACK with Bob Larson," during the Christmas holiday season. A desperate listener can find hope and help by dialing 1-800-821-TALK. Our slogan is, "Meeting the needy at the point of their need." From David's opening comments, there was no question he qualified.

"TALK-BACK with Bob Larson" is aired in nearly two hundred cities, including twenty of the top twenty-five North American markets. The show provides a forum for controversial issues seldom discussed elsewhere in the media. Satanism is one of those subjects.

David expressed his point harshly. "I don't believe in Christmas. I'm a Satanist. How can you celebrate the birth of Jesus when he was a criminal dying for his crimes?"

"What crime is it to love people, to die for them, to shed your blood for them?" I asked.

9

"I've bled for the devil," David responded calmly. "I've cut myself. I've also offered Satan the blood sacrifices of animals. To show my dedication to the devil, I've carved pentagrams and upside-down crosses on my arms."

"How did you do that?"

"With razor blades and propane torches."

I kept probing David for more information, trying to discover how deeply he was dedicated to the devil. This knowledge would help me decide how to direct the conversation to counsel him.

"What else have you done for the devil?"

"Well," David answered, "I play in a black metal band called Eternal Death."

"What do you sing about?"

" 'Unholy Rites' is one of the songs I've written. It's about sex with corpses," David told me. "Our satanic group digs up bodies in the graveyard."

"How did you hear this show?" I wondered out loud.

"I was just flipping through the radio dial and heard you talking about Slayer. They're my favorite rock band. I heard you're going to be on tour with them next week."

"How did you start listening to Slayer?"

"When I was young, Slayer brought Satanism into my life. It's because of their music that I worship the devil. Their lyrics introduced me to Lord Satan. They made me what I am. The words of their songs are the most important thing to me.

"A lot of other kids are like me. Slayer fans think the band members are gods. They worship them like crazy. If you want my advice, you'd better not go on tour with them. You might get hurt if their fans find out who you are.

"One more thing," David added. "Ask them if they're really Satanists, 'cause if they're not, they're phony and I'm not going to listen to them anymore."

STALKING SLAYER

A few days before David's call, my secretary had buzzed my office intercom to convey an unusual invitation.

"Bob Guccione, Jr., publisher of the rock magazine *Spin*, is on the phone," she said. "He wants you to fly to West Germany and tour with Slayer so you can write a cover story for *Spin*. Will you take the call?"

"He wants what?" I was astonished. It was hard to believe the son of *Penthouse's* publisher, who was also the publisher of his own highly successful rock periodical, would ask me to tour as a journalist with the most notorious black metal band in the world.

Guccione and I had gotten to know each other well in recent years, an odd couple if ever there was one. He has a heritage of porn publications. I am a Christian talk show host.

We first met when "TALK-BACK" was doing a series of shows about the report of the Attorney General's Commission on Pornography. Guccione was my guest to debate those who wanted warning stickers on record albums with questionable lyrics. He was a repeat guest on several subsequent occasions when "TALK-BACK" discussed rock music.

This time, Guccione was inviting me to be his guest for an all-expense paid trip to West Germany. That part was intriguing. What perplexed me was touring with Slayer.

"Guccione, what are you trying to do to me?" I kidded.

"The staff of *Spin* thinks it's a great idea. It's the ultimate irony, you and Slayer. We originally thought about sending you on tour with a black metal band called Death. But they weren't bad enough. Slayer has the worst reputation as a satanic metal band.

"Everything is cleared with their manager and record company. We've told them this will be a *Spin* feature story. You'll have artistic freedom to write what you want."

The idea was mind-boggling. Me, writing a cover story for one of America's top rock magazines. Me, on tour with a band that sings about necrophilia and lyrically declares, "Praise Satan." A once-in-a-lifetime opportunity to go behind the scenes on a rock 'n' roll tour.

"You'll have an all-access pass to go anywhere you want with the band," Guccione promised. "Backstage, in the dressing room, on the bus, in the audience, even on stage.

"Will you do it?" Guccione wanted to know.

I thought about David and other teenage callers, like Lars whom you'll meet in Chapter 6. They all said that their fascination with Satanism had started with Slayer. Here was a unique opportunity to get the facts.

"OK," I agreed. "Tell me when and where to meet Slayer."

"You'll leave Friday the 13th for Hamburg via Frankfurt. Don't let them sacrifice you on an altar to Satan," Guccione joked.

Friday the 13th, I thought to myself. *Hmmm.*

Seventy-two hours later, I was on my way to meet the boys in the band who sing, "Warriors from the gates of hell . . . In Lord Satan we trust."

Is Slayer serious about Satan? I wondered. *Do they look forward to partying with the evil one in the eternal inferno?*

I soon found out. That night in Hamburg I saw my first Slayer concert, and all hell broke loose.

HELL IN HAMBURG

To chants of "Slayer, Slayer," the band came on stage, appropriately dressed in black. Guitarist Kerry King wore a leather shin guard embedded with steel studs in the form of an inverted cross. Guitarist Jeff Hanneman sported a tee shirt saying, "Slaytanic Wehrmacht" (war machine). Drummer Dave Lombardo wore a tank top and shorts. Vocalist Tom Araya's tee shirt declared, "Sex, Murder, Art."

Slayer picked a poor place to play for the devil. The hall was cavernous and cold. It had a thirty foot ceiling and no heat. Inside, the temperature was about fifty degrees. Backstage, Slayer shivered, hunkered down like four lost sheep far from home.

Moments later on stage, they became fire-breathing demons from rock 'n' roll hell. In the midst of fog machines and the thunderous roar of three thousand fans, they exuded the embodiment of evil. They must have practiced for hours in front of mirrors to effect their snarls of contempt for decency.

"Guten Nacht!" Araya yelled, attempting a little German.

The fans roared approval. He could have spoken Swahili for all they cared. Slayer fans weren't there for small talk. They wanted to hear the songs of Satan sung syllable for syllable, note for note, just like on their records. The fans lip-synched the words, although the majority had no idea what they were saying.

No one in the band appeared nervous. They had obviously been through this a zillion times. The lighting man played his big board like a virtuoso pianist. First, the blue light on Araya, then the yellow spot on King. Next, Hanneman stepped to the foot of the stage at a spot marked "X," one of many locations on the floor where masking tape was pasted to show members of the band where to stand for the right spotlight. A red spot shone upward under Hanneman's chin, creating eerie shadows, as he glowered menacingly.

The audience scowled back. They were a beer-buzzed, wasted bunch that the band referred to backstage as "German vermin." Their metal regalia openly invited evil. There were thousands of jean jackets, backs emblazoned with demonic depictions: horned goat-man (baphomet) symbols of Satan, gruesome images of devils, and more upside-down crosses than a denizen of demons could concoct in a month. One strange picture on the back of a jean jacket depicted a naked woman lying on her back, legs spread apart at the junction of an inverted crucifix. Black magic pentagrams declared, "Welcome to hell." Where else would Lucifer feel more welcome?

Behind Slayer, centered above the drummer, the stage backdrop featured their stylized pentagram logo. On either side of the satanic symbol were two six foot stained-glass windows superimposed with a cross—upside down, of course.

The group began with "Hell Awaits." "Jesus knows your soul cannot be saved," they sang. "Crucify the so-called Lord!"

Next they sang "Black Magic," in which they claimed to be "captive of a force of Satan's might . . . Death takes my hand and captures my soul."

Later songs, such as "Evil Has No Boundaries," were overt invocations to the devil: "Satan our master in evil mayhem guides us with every first step."

No wonder teens like Dave began to worship Satan after playing these songs over and over again on their Walkmans and ghetto blasters.

The deafening roar of 120 decibels (112 is the pain threshold) was like standing next to a jet taking off. Slayer launched into "Spill the Blood": "Spill your blood, let it run on to me. Take my hand and let go of your life . . . You've spilt the blood. I have your soul."

How odd that the madness of black metal mania would strike in West Germany, a country that once boasted Europe's richest cultural heritage, the land of Bach and Beethoven. Before the parents of Slayer fans were born, however, Nazi insanity unleashed an on-slaught of evil that knew no reasonable bounds. Demagogic rallies and sterile architecture promoted the Aryan ideal. Mass psychology triumphed over reason.

Clearly, Slayer's brand of black metal music was breeding the same insensitivity to logic. For the Nazis, it was the swastika. For Slayer, the pentagram. Another symbol of evil was once again inciting legions of the discontented to overthrow an existing order. What other conclusion could I draw, hearing Slayer sing "Altar of Sacrifice," which described the human sacrifice of a virgin with lines like, "Satan's slaughter, ceremonial death. Answer his every command. Enter to the realm of Satan . . . Learn the sacred words of praise, 'Hail Satan.'"

Fifty years ago Germans goose-stepped in exacting regimentation, stiff-armed salutes sanctifying der Führer. In Hamburg I watched German metal maniacs thrust satanic salutes upward and slam-dance to the fastest rhythms in rock. Their favorite was "Angel of Death," about Joseph Mengele, the butcher of Auschwitz, whom Slayer described as the "Sadist surgeon of demise, sadist of the noblest blood . . . Monarch to the Kingdom of the Dead." The song was an explicit account of Mengele's machinations. The crowd reacted violently.

In front of the stage was a location called the pit, a five-foot-wide section between the stage and steel restraining bars that held back the crazed crowds. One by one, various members of the audience headed for the pit. Fans at Slayer concerts don't sit because there aren't any chairs. They stand the whole night. Occasionally, one of them leaps into the air and somehow lands on top of the audience. Heads, shoulders, and outstretched hands support him. Gradually, he makes his way forward, pushing or being pushed. Crawling on his back and stomach, he surges forward like a fullback vaulting defenders at a goal line stand.

Eventually, he lunges toward the pit. Head over heels he somersaults the last few feet until he lands head or feet first in the pit. Then security personnel ungraciously escort him to the side of the auditorium. He's sent to the back of the crowd to try the same thing again.

Throughout the concert, the fans frowned constantly. Their expressions were intensely evil—except when I took their pictures. Then the tension in their facial muscles seemed to relax. They smiled. No one heard me say cheese, but the sight of a camera caught them off guard, and for a brief moment they appeared to forget where they were. After the flash went off, something seemed to click, and their eyes would narrow again. Curling their lips in contempt of propriety, they'd return to their devilish demeanor.

Everything Slayer did appeared contrived, even their on-stage banter. During the next days, I would learn that every comment of Slayer was canned. Night after night, they did the same introductions to song. Nothing was spontaneous. Even Araya's right eyelid, which arched slightly when he said "Satan," looked like it had been choreographed. Every note of every riff, every scowl was the same, on cue, at the right bar.

Does Anton LaVey of the Church of Satan look this bored when he celebrates his umpteenth black mass? I wondered.

When the concert ended, the band strutted off stage where the tour manager handed them towels to wipe off profuse sweat. Then they went directly to their home on wheels. No conversation, few autographs, and little time wasted.

A rock 'n' roll tour is an exercise in opposites. You sleep all day and go all night. Concerts end about 11:00 P.M. Then the bus rolls on to the next town, usually a four- to six-hour drive. About six o'clock the next morning, the band goes to bed. At precisely two o'clock in the afternoon, the tour manager gives everyone a wake-up call. An hour later, taxis are summoned to take the band to the concert hall for sound checks and pre-concert activities. After the show, the routine starts again.

Slayer's glorified Winnebago was somewhat luxurious, if contemporary K-Mart is your style. Two TVs, two VCRs, and a supply of videos, mostly horror flicks. Also on board was a bathroom, a microwave to heat after-concert catered meals, and a center lounge to relax. In the back were six bunks, where anyone not prone to motion sickness could sack out. Since watching endless films of Chuck Norris and Bruce Lee is not my idea of entertainment, I chose one of the bed-on-wheels cubicles.

All through the night, I heard endless banter.

"How many hours until we get to the hotel?"

"Ice, where's the ice? They're supposed to bring ice on board the bus every night. You just can't get ice in Europe."

"Boy, did we have problems staying in tune tonight."

"Driver, could you stop the bus so we can get some postcards to send our girlfriends back home?"

The Slayer fans I've talked with on my radio show think the band indulges in an endless orgy of devotion to the devil. In truth, Slayer was pampered, bored, and anxious to get home. They wanted to buy picture postcards of castles on the Rhine, not black candles and sacred daggers to summon demons.

"Just nineteen days left," Kerry King said to me. "As soon as I got off the plane in Frankfurt to begin the tour, I started counting the days until we could go home."

THE BIG "S" QUESTION

During the last few days of the tour, I spent time alone with each member of the band, probing his spiritual beliefs. That's when I got to the big "S" question: "Are you Satanists?"

Drummer Dave Lombardo resembled the kid next door, the one you'd want your daughter to marry if he weren't already happily hitched. He wasn't comfortable with the band's satanic overtones. "Look," he said. "I didn't write those lyrics. I wasn't in favor of using an upside down cross as a stage backdrop. I just want to be the best metal drummer in the business." Dave is the only Slayer with an occult background of sorts. His Roman Catholic, Cuban-born family dabbled in the Caribbean cult of Santeria. Somehow he retained his reverence for God, probably because of a Catholic school education.

Lead vocalist Tom Araya is a mystery. Born in Chili, he came to the United States at five years of age. His face persistently glows with mischievous malevolence. Unlike the others, he won't state whether he's a current or past Satanist. His eyes twinkle at the "S" question, as though he's hiding some dark secret of the soul or cleverly milking the mystique.

Araya is an incurable pessimist. "The world is going to end in disaster soon," he said seriously. "I feel it wherever I go." Ironically, both his parents are devout Christians and charismatic lay preachers. "My mother prays for me every night," he said.

Guitarist Jeff Hanneman seemed most uncomfortable being questioned about his personal beliefs. He bristled at the mere mention of involvement with Satan. Jeff wasn't even sure what a Satanist does or believes. To him, the whole thing is ridiculous, and all religion is "stupid."

So why does he write lyrics like, "Lucifer takes my dark soul down to the fiery pits of hell?" Why do his eyes flash on stage with an aggressive, almost demonic intensity, exhorting the crowd to ever more expressive states of frenzy?

Jeff admitted that something in his childhood had angered him. "The stage is my opportunity to release that unresolved aggression," he freely acknowledged.

Guitarist Kerry King also admitted to writing some pretty "sick" lyrics. Case in point, the song "Necrophiliac": "I feel the urge, the growing need to f*** this sinful corpse. My task's complete, the bitch's soul lies raped in demonic lust."

But Kerry King said he'd rather spend his time at home in Phoenix with his four dogs and dozens of snakes. He breeds the slimy critters professionally. Diamondback python babies fetch one thousand dollars each, he gleefully informed me. Kerry claimed he'd never read the Bible, though he said if he did he'd probably write some Iron Maiden-type lyrics from the Revelation. He looked once at *The Satanic Bible*, but found it boring and trashed it. Kerry said horror movies are his main source of song inspiration.

Before leaving to tour with Slayer, I had made a cassette recording of my conversation with David, my "TALK-BACK" caller. One night in Nuremberg, I played it for Jeff, Tom, and Kerry. Bluntly, I asked if they assumed any guilt for Dave's dilemma.

"It's the parents' responsibility to be aware of what their children are doing," Araya argued. "It's not our job. We're just poets and musicians."

Kerry added, "Every album we've put out has a sticker about objectionable language, so it's not our fault."

What they said angered me. David had put his life on the line for the devil, and he credited Slayer's image and lyrics with selling Satanism to him. That may not be what the members of the band intended, but they didn't regret their influence on David's spiritual condition. Some would call it passing the buck. In Nuremberg after World War II, Nazi war criminals called it "just following orders."

I asked Jeff, Tom, and Kerry if they had anything to say to David. Showing them my tape recorder, I said, "This kid is really messed up, and you're his heroes. Could you record a message to David that would encourage him to get out of Satanism and find some help for his problems? I'll be sure he hears what you say."

They refused.

Why? They argued it wasn't their problem. They didn't want to get involved. They repeated their premise that David's parents should help him. He should see a professional counselor. The list of excuses droned on and on.

The members of Slayer, who had so carefully crafted evil lyrics glorifying Satan worship, weren't willing to say one encouraging word to a misguided teenager who really believed they meant what they said in their songs. Doing so would risk demolishing their image, and that would mean fewer record sales, concert tickets, and less money. When you're the kings of black metal music, you don't abdicate, even when a life is at stake. Somewhere, I could hear Lucifer laughing.

Perhaps they didn't offer answers for David's dilemma because they had no solutions for their own spiritual problems. Tom Araya admitted he would write lyrics about anything except love. "We did a remake of 'In-A-Gada-Da-Vida,' and I changed the words 'I love you' to 'I want you,' meant in a sexual fashion. I don't feel comfortable writing about love," he said.

Slayer is not a band of hope. You can't dance to the music, and you wouldn't want to live by it. They're convinced the world is headed for an apocalypse soon. "Eat, drink, and be merry. That's what I'm doing," said Kerry King.

Does any kind of altruism fit into Slayer's scheme of existence?

"I matter to myself," King commented. "I don't get in anybody else's face if they don't get into mine first."

BLACK METAL AND MAMMON

The love of money is the root of all kinds of evil according to the

Bible.[1] If Slayer's soul was sold to Satan, they did so at the bank, not at a black mass. The forbidden brew Slayer sipped isn't the drink of lyrical death and despair. It's the elixir of fame. In the Garden of Rock 'n' Roll, they ate the apple of image over ingenuity, hype over integrity.

Their root of evil is rock stardom. Their pact of iniquity is with the pop music charts and concert paraphernalia sales. One fan in Bonn, West Germany proudly showed me his tee shirt. He smugly spread his arms and threw open his jacket to reveal the pentagram on the front. It said, "Satan's Army."

That's how fans like David see themselves, as an elite division of soul-slayers, trampling underfoot all that is decent and good. They buy into the band's image and hold Slayer hostage to an idea Araya and Company dreamed up seven years ago to achieve rock stardom. Privately, the band admits their reputation of being Satanists is worn-out. But if they changed direction, David and all those other kids in Satan's army would feel betrayed. So Slayer keeps pasting those same sneers on their faces night after night, looking for ever more gruesome subjects to pan off on the ignorant.

The members of Slayer kept telling me how much they cared about their fans and how hard they worked as a band to play the music kids liked. But what's an hour on stage worth to a teenager who has been spurned by parents and society? Doesn't the message of an upside-down cross and the atmosphere of evil say more?

DAVID AND THE DEVIL

"The members of Slayer are not Satanists," I informed David when I returned from the tour. "I was with them all last week. Their songs about Satan are only a gimmick."

"That makes me mad. If they're phony, they're not going to be my main band anymore," David answered angrily, obviously disappointed.

David renounced Slayer. Their hypocrisy of performing one way and living another turned him off.

Yet the most interesting aspect of David's story wasn't his fascination with Slayer and black metal music. It was how his parents ignored his fascination with evil.

David's arms were scarred with pentagrams and inverted crosses. He played in a rock band called Eternal Death. Because he wanted to do a human sacrifice and others in his coven refused, David was kicked out of his own Satanist group.

What father and mother could overlook blatant engrossment with the occult in view of such symptoms of Satanism?

When I asked David, he responded quickly, "My parents think it's a phase I'm going through. But they're wrong. It's my religion!"

I asked David if I could send him a Bible so he could become acquainted with an alternative viewpoint about life. His response was chilling.

"I burn Bibles," David said. "When I don't burn them, I tear out the pages, chew, and swallow them, then puke them back up."

"What about Satanists who renounce devil worship? You've heard some of them on 'TALK-BACK.' What do you think of them?" I asked.

"Thanks for getting those wimps out of Satanism," David responded. "You're helping our religion. We only want the strong and true."

WILL YOU ACCEPT SLAYER'S CHALLENGE?

Slayer's challenge to parents was their way of passing the buck. But parents can't ignore the gauntlet they tossed down. Neither can anyone responsible for molding the lives of today's young people. Teenagers are searching for unconditional love. If they wander into evil ways, they must know you will respond quickly with alarm and concern.

The heart of this book is for parents, grandparents, guardians, teachers, youth counselors, and other mentors of America's youth. Slayer's summons, "It's the parents' responsibility," challenges everyone who guides young lives. This book may make you uncomfortable, but it could be the antidote to evil for someone you love.

I'm acutely conscious of the many teens like David who have sworn allegiance to Satan and have been inducted into a bond of unholy loyalty. Please read on to see why they have exchanged the divine for the diabolical. Before they kill or are killed, discover how to tell them who calls the shots and who's in control.

Together, we will expose evil from the seamy to the sinister. And we'll see why evil entices rather than repels. Most importantly, we'll understand how to lovingly rescue those who sell themselves to Satan and become the devil's disciples on an altar of sacrifice.

Murder for the Devil

"They burned my girlfriend alive while I watched. She wasn't the only one they killed. Another friend of mine was forced to say 'Satan, I give my life to you now,' as they pushed him over a cliff."

Sarah was petrified. "I've never told anyone before," she confessed.

Why? Her answer was simple.

"What I saw was so inconceivable, no one would believe me!"

But fourteen-year-old Sarah did tell me. Calling a talk show and giving a fictitious name allowed Sarah the anonymity she needed, even if millions heard her story of enslavement to Satanism. Sarah had discovered that teens like David, the caller in the first chapter, sometimes fulfill their pledge to murder for the devil.

"How did they burn your girlfriend?" I asked.

"They tied her to a platform and lit a fire under her," she explained.

"Didn't she cry for help?" I wanted to know.

"She screamed, but no one would put out the flames. They were all wearing masks so no one could see who they were," Sarah sobbed.

"What did you do while all this was going on?"

Sarah continued. "I tried to stop them, but they held me back. They made me watch and then beat me up afterwards."

Sarah's involvement with Satanism started with drugs, heavy

metal music, and various forms of anti-social behavior. She did pot, speed, LSD, any drug she could get her hands on. She slept with every guy who would have sex with her. Soon the friend who was eventually burned alive invited her to a party, which turned out to be a satanic ritual. At first, it was an electrifying departure from her strict Christian upbringing.

Sarah didn't realize that killing a few animals preceded human torture and murder. The sight of seeing someone incinerated alive was so horrifying she later attempted suicide three times. Sarah was too terrified to talk about her brush with Satanism until the day she dialed me.

"No one knows what I've seen," she divulged. "I was flipping across the dial and heard your show. I called because I can't live with the memories any longer."

Sarah knew I wouldn't dismiss her amazing episodes as fantasy. She hadn't gone to the police because there was no proof. Of the two sacrifices she had seen, one body was charred beyond recognition and the other was drowned in the sea below a cliff. No traces. No evidence. Who would believe a teenager with a history of drug abuse?

"The burning sacrifice was reported in the newspapers," she acknowledged. "It was near some houses, and someone must have heard the screaming. But they never found who did it."

Why did I believe Sarah? With slight alterations, I had heard the same story from dozens of other youngsters. The similarities were singular. Gradual induction into the cult. Horrifying ceremonies designed to instill terror, guilt, and silence. Killings too bloody to imagine. No witnesses. No signs of the crime.

"Why haven't you told your parents?" I asked Sarah.

Her answer was a typical teen response. "I never tell them anything," she answered. "My parents and I never talk."

Don't imagine Sarah's tragedy couldn't happen to a child you know. Her parents are respected Christians in positions of church leadership. They are totally unaware of their daughter's involvement in Satanism. They only know Sarah is rebellious and suicidal. Like most parents whose children explore the occult, they are excluded from Sarah's murky world of evil atrocities. They aren't alone. Even those whose job it is to investigate and prosecute crime are often in the dark about the devil's deeds.

SLEUTHING SATANIC SLAYINGS

Many law enforcement authorities ignore signs of occult crime—headless hens, spray-painted graffiti, decapitated animals, and mutilated bodies. But the times, "they are a changin'". According to *Newsweek* magazine,[1] an informal network of approximately one thousand officers and counselors tracks satanic crimes via phone, newsletters, and seminars. In his book *The Ultimate Evil*, author Maury Terry writes, "There is compelling evidence of the existence of a nationwide network of satanic cults, some branched into child pornography and violent sadomasochistic crime, including murder. I am concerned that the toll of innocent victims will steadily mount unless law enforcement officials recognize the threat and face it."[2]

You may remember some of the murderers I am going to analyze, yet you may not know the satanic involvement of these criminals. Until recently, felonies committed for the devil went unrecognized or were treated as the actions of a psychopathic deviant. The idea of organized satanic groups dedicated to violence and vandalism has largely been ignored by investigators and prosecutors.

CHARLES MANSON

There has been much to monitor in the short history of slaying for Satan. Some say the current craze started August 9 and 10, 1969, the nights Charles Manson and his "family" of followers murdered seven victims, including actress Sharon Tate. Apparently Manson had been seduced by an ideology suggesting Christ and Satan, no longer adversaries, had reconciled. Thus, worshipping Satan is the same as acquiescing to Christ. Charles Manson borrowed his insane ideas from Robert DeGrimston, founder of the Process Church, a sixties street cult.

According to Manson's prosecutor, Vincent Bugliosi, both Manson and DeGrimston preached "an imminent, violent Armageddon, in which all but the chosen few would be destroyed." As Bugliosi describes it, Manson slightly altered the Process theology that Jehovah, Lucifer, and Christ are all reconciled. "Manson had a simpler duality; he was known to his followers as both Satan and Christ," Bugliosi believes.[3]

THE NIGHT STALKER

In 1985, Californians locked their doors as the terrifying Night Stalker case dragged on for months. Residents feared they and their families would become victims of satanically-inspired rape and murder. At least fourteen victims had been slain, and many more were robbed and sodomized by the Stalker. His victims were usually residents of yellow houses near freeways.

The Stalker's methods amplified the horror. In one particularly ghoulish slaying, the victim's eyes were gouged out. The Stalker often drew pentagrams at the crime scene. The wife of one of his victims declared he had forced her to "swear on Satan" not to scream for help. He favored no one. The Night Stalker molested children, murdered men and women, and used both guns and knives. Typically, his heinous work was done between midnight and 6:00 A.M., when he sneaked into darkened homes through unlocked doors and windows.

Police eventually arrested twenty-eight-year-old Richard Ramirez of El Paso, Texas. At his arraignment, Ramirez grinned and raised his arm to reveal an inked pentagram in the palm of his hand. Friends of Ramirez claimed he was fascinated with the music and satanic symbolism of the Australian rock group AC/DC. At a Rosemead, California condominium Ramirez allegedly murdered thirty-four-year-old Dayle Okazaki and left behind a baseball cap emblazoned with the AC/DC logo.

The cover of the jacket for the AC/DC album "Highway to Hell" depicts the lead singer with satanic horns protruding from his head. He holds in his hands a devilishly pointed tail. To investigators, AC/DC's song "Night Prowler" is chillingly similar to the activities of Ramirez. The tune vividly describes a murderer lurking at night. "You won't feel the steel until it's hanging out your back," the lyrics warn. Sounding like a police profile of Ramirez, the refrain suggests, "I am your night prowler, I sleep in the day . . . Suspended animation, as I slip into your room." After depicting the terror of a victim awaiting a homicidal attack, the singer says, "There ain't nothing you can do."

Ramirez's association with the occult was more than a passing fascination. He drew a satanic star on the upper part of his arm. Donna Myers, who knew Ramirez and eventually helped police finger him for the crimes, says he also etched a witch's star on his stomach. According to Myers, "He would say Satan is a supreme being, like we worship God. He would tell me that Satan watches over him, so he doesn't get caught or hurt."[4]

RICKY KASSO

The heinous criminal activities of adults like Manson and Ramirez were soon adopted by younger deviants like Ricky Kasso of Northport, New York, a Long Island suburb. With his blond hair and blue eyes, Kasso could have been the kid next door. As an adolescent, he was an avid athlete, fond of early morning football practices. But at seventeen, he was underweight with slurred speech and no short-term memory. In his father's words, "All he thought about was drugs and rock music."[5] Kasso and his friends formed a self-styled, devil-worshiping cult they called the Knights of the Black Circle. On signs and walls, they spray-painted upside-down crosses, 666 to represent the Antichrist, inverted stars symbolizing the devil, and names of metal rock stars like Ozzy and Black Sabbath.

Kasso scared his mother by smearing ketchup on his wrists, declaring she had driven him to suicide. He once wrote a song called "A Child of the Devil." Ricky's frightened parents told doctors about his suicide attempts, threatening behavior, use of hallucinogens, and arrest for digging up a grave. He was judged to be "antisocial" but not "psychotic."[6] A friend thought otherwise. He declared, "Ricky would talk to the devil. He said the devil came to him in the form of a tree, which sprouted out of the ground and glowed."[7]

Ricky Kasso exemplifies what happens when authorities fail to take serious note of satanic symbols and paraphernalia. For three years, Northport police had been finding remains of tortured or charred animals that appeared to have been victims of ritual sacrifice. The neglect to pinpoint the source of such deviltry eventually led to the murder of seventeen-year-old Gary Lauwers.

Kasso blamed Lauwers for stealing from him $100 worth of PCP, the drug known as angel dust. With the help of an accomplice, eighteen-year-old James Toriano, Ricky tortured his victim for three hours. Lauwers was stabbed seventeen times, then Kasso gouged out his eyes while forcing him to say, "I love you, Satan." After his arrest, Kasso hung himself in his jail cell to his cellmates' chants of "Hang up! Hang up!"

In the cases of Kasso and many other youths involved in murder for the devil, Satanism is far from an organized system of allegiance to Lucifer. Disaffected teenagers feel a sense of importance in Satanism. It is the paramount perversion of all their parents hold dear, the ultimate rebellion. Satanism is a supreme cry for help, directed toward a society that gives youth everything materially, but no meaning for life.

SATAN'S SONS AND DAUGHTERS

Teenagers today grow up in a world saturated with satanic symbols and suggestions—black metal music, Dungeons & Dragons, horror movies, occult emblems, and diabolical paraphernalia. Some parents mistakenly assume it's harmless, that kids will grow out of it. That's what David's parents in Chapter 1 thought. "After all," parents muse, "we did some pretty strange things when we were young."

The devil? He's merely a justification for youthful mischievousness. From getting drunk to doing drugs, "The devil made me do it" is the ultimate excuse. If that's your conclusion as a parent, you're skating on thin ice over a hot hell.

As host of America's most listened-to talk show for more than six years, I've encountered many kids who credit Satan as the inspiration for their outrageous conduct. Over the air while millions listened, teens have told me of incredible abuse and unimaginable evil. The malevolence they reveal involves more than a few marijuana joints and reckless vandalism.

Bobbie was inducted into occult pornography and forced to commit bestiality. Damius (an occult name) participated in human sacrifices. Nicki placed curses on those who attempted to interfere with her worship of Satan. Lee claimed to engage in sexual intercourse with female spirit beings. Andrew built a satanic altar in his basement with idols of the devil and voodoo gods. You'll meet other teenagers like them in later chapters of this book. These are real people with real stories of inconceivable iniquity. Do teens who swear allegiance to Satan have something in common?

As a result of my on-the-air conversations and my personal counseling with teens off the air, a profile of those inclined toward Satanism has emerged. Many are from broken homes where they were neglected or ignored. Most are extraordinarily bright and sensitive. Each harbors a deep, hidden hurt, often sexual or physical abuse. Generally, they have experienced disappointment with organized Christianity. Turning to the devil isn't their first choice. Suicidally inclined and overcome with a sense of worthlessness, they see Satan as their last resort to grasp a sense of personal importance.

How had Sarah nearly become a daughter of the devil? Her parents divorced when she was a child, and she currently sees her biological father only once a year. Her youthful curiosity, fueled by parental indifference, propelled her into post-pubescent crisis.

Sarah's situation was put into perspective when she asked me a rhetorical question. "You want to know how a stoner, rocker, hooker, Satanist bitch could come from such a good family?" she queried.

"I could say it was rebellion or demons that did it," she responded. "But it was my parents who drove me over the edge. My real father doesn't love me, and my stepfather doesn't have time for me. My mother acts like I don't exist. All she does is yell at me when she finds out I've done something wrong."

I pondered, *How many who have murdered for the devil felt like Sarah, but had no one who cared enough to hear their frustrations?*

Charles Manson, Richard Ramirez, Ricky Kasso, and other killers for Satan were not born bad. They were bent bad by a society that neglected their basic human needs and substituted affluence for affection. In defiance, they became Satanists, determined to exploit evil and get forcibly what they couldn't receive freely from those who should have loved them. A lack of self-esteem was the chief reason they exchanged virtue for evil. If being good didn't bring happiness, then being bad, exceedingly bad, would at least lead to power and lustful satisfaction.

SIGNS OF SATANISM

If you work with teenagers or are the parent of a teen, your first question is probably, "How do I know if a teen is involved with Satanism?"

Some telltale signs of youthful involvement in Satanism are:

• An unhealthy preoccupation with fantasy role-playing games like Dungeons & Dragons (D&D).

• An interest in Ouija boards and other occult games.

• A preoccupation with psychic phenomena like telepathy, astral projection, Tarot cards, I Ching, and parapsychology.

• An addiction to horror movies like the "Friday the 13th" and "Nightmare on Elm Street" series, whose main characters kill and maim.

• An obsession with heavy metal music, particularly black metal bands like Slayer, Venom, Ozzy, Metallica, Megadeth, King Diamond, and other groups that evoke satanic symbolism.

• An affinity for satanic paraphernalia, including posters of black metal bands, skulls, knives, chalices, black candles, and robes.

• An inclination to write poems or letters about Satanism or to sketch designs of upside-down crosses, pentagrams, the number 666, names of the devil, or skulls and other symbols of death.

• An attraction to satanic literature and such books as *The Satanic Bible*, the *Necronomicon*, the writings of Aleister Crowley, or keeping a private journal such as a *Book of Shadows* (a self-designed secret chronicle of satanic activities and ideas).

• An involvement with friends who dress in black, greet each other with the satanic salute (index and pinkie finger extended, with palm facing inward), speak and write backwards, or organize secret meetings.

This list is by no means exhaustive, but it does categorize some of the more common satanic signs of those dabbling in devil worship. Before you dismiss any of these indicators as not applicable to a child you know, remember the error of overlooking such curiosities, as did the parents of David.

Beware of the temptation to search a child's room or screen his mail, which would breach his trust in you. Don't suddenly demand that every offensive poster come off his wall and every distasteful record album go to the garbage. Precipitous action will instill further anger and rebellion. Instead, be alert for additional clues of satanic involvement. Ask prudent questions of your child's peers, teachers, and acquaintances. Above all, don't assume Satanism can't intrude upon your family.

In the second part of this book, "The Selling of Satanism," we will look at the significance regarding each sign of satanic interest I mentioned above. We will see how frequently these telltale signals of Satanism appeared in the lives of teenagers who committed satanic crimes and teenagers enmeshed in the occult who called "TALK-BACK." We'll also give suggestions for parents and counselors who want to help youth resist these influences. (Teenagers reading the book may wish to skip some sections at the end of each chapter, which are intended to advise parents regarding Satanism and their children.)

In the third part, "Dancing with the Devil," we'll look at the direct influence Satanism has on teenagers. We'll examine satanic rituals and practices so concerned adults can be better informed about the diabolical temptations faced by today's teens. The existence of killing cults and their rites of sacrifice will also be surveyed. Eighteen-year-old Sean Sellers, the youngest inmate on death row in the Oklahoma State penitentiary, will tell us about his involvement in Satanism and suggest some ways that parents and counselors can reach kids like himself.

Then in the fourth section, "The Roots of Satanism," we'll scrutinize the philosophy of Satanism by examining the beliefs of organized satanic churches. We'll also investigate the theological roots of demonic beliefs espoused by well-known Satanist Aleister Crowley and organized occult folk religions, such as voodoo, macumba, and witchcraft. Finally, we'll inspect the occult literature that motivates teenage satanic beliefs, including *The Satanic Bible* and other black magic volumes.

In conclusion, we'll compare the theology of Satanism with Christianity and other world religions concerning good and evil. Nearly every day on "TALK-BACK" I confront the ideology of evil purported by Satanism. I want you to understand the roots of this satanic system so you too can effectively combat its lures and lies.

Do not underestimate the extent to which Satanism has invaded our youth culture. According to Shane Westhoelter, president of the National Information Network, 30 to 40 percent of high school students are involved in some form of the occult. Westhoelter also contends that up to 70 percent of all crimes committed by teens under the age of seventeen are motivated by involvement in the occult.[8]

The Chicago-based Cult Awareness Network concurs regarding the significance of teenage Satanism. At least 10 percent of the 250 calls received by the Network each month are about satanic cults, a significant figure considering the thousands of American cults. Cynthia Kisser, Executive Director, suspects far more youngsters are devil worshipers. Cynthia says, "I believe for every one we're hearing about, there are five or six teenagers we haven't picked up on."[9]

The purpose of this book is to awaken you to the seriousness of teenage Satanism. Restless young souls are seeking hearing hearts that will listen to their fears. If you fail to acknowledge their pleadings, they will find someone else to heed their hurt. Before evil knocks at the door of their lives, show them how to let love in.

PART TWO

The Selling of Satanism

Occult Enticements

"Hi, Bob. I called your radio show today because I want to talk to you about playing Bloody Mary. Do you know anything about it?"

"Sure," I answered. "But most of my listeners don't. Describe it to them."

The explanation that followed was incredible, and all the more so because it was coming from a twelve-year-old boy named Chad.

"Well," Chad said, "you go into a dark bathroom, stare into the mirror, and chant, 'Bloody Mary, Bloody Mary.' You wait until invisible claws scratch your face and you bleed. That's how you know Bloody Mary is there. Now my friend Jamie and me are into more exotic stuff. We go through the mirror."

That was a new one. "Have you ever heard of astral-projection or out-of-the-body experiences?" I asked.

"Yeah, it's like that," Chad responded. "I look into the mirror and do the Bloody Mary chant. Then my mind goes into the mirror and travels to my friend Jamie's house. I got the idea from the movie 'Poltergeist.'"

"Does Jamie know when you're there?" I wondered aloud.

"Yes, if he does the right chants too. Sometimes I visit him when he doesn't know it, and I tell him later what I saw him doing."

"Chad, I want to ask you an important question. When you leave your body, who guards your soul while you're gone?"

Chad didn't know.

"There are two ways evil can overtake your soul," I said. "One is

35

for you to sell your soul to Satan. The other is for you to do something in the occult that leaves your soul unprotected. When you leave your body, your consciousness isn't there to resist evil. When you visit Jamie, something else could invade your soul."

Chad was startled. He thought Bloody Mary was a lot of fun, a cute trick borrowed from Hollywood. The idea of the devil had never occurred to him. That's the way it is with most people. Casual clashes with the occult are commonplace in a society satiated with spiritism.

We'll begin exploring the selling of Satanism by considering some less obvious enticements. These are influences that parents, teachers, and youth counselors might never think are harmful. That unsuspecting evaluation is the enchantment by which many teens are trapped.

THE INDUCEMENT OF PSYCHIC PHENOMENA

For all the bad press Nancy Reagan got over her attention to astrology, it appears she had company along the Potomac. Congressman Charlie Ross (D-N.C.), who promotes the paranormal in Washington, D.C., says, "At any given time, about one-fourth of the members of Congress are actively interested in PSI [an acronym for psychic phenomena], healing, prophecy, remote viewing, or physical manifestations of psychic power."

Senator Claiborne Pell (D-R.I.), chairman of the Senate Foreign Relations Committee, is a vocal advocate of psychic research. The bookcase in Pell's private Capitol office is crammed with occult volumes, including *The Astral Body* and the works of Shirley MacLaine. He admits consulting mediums to communicate with dead relatives.[1]

The Pentagon underwrites classified psychic research, and the CIA has used psychics to spy on Soviet weaponry. General Manuel Noriega, Panama's dictator, was the subject of governmental paranormal sleuthing. Some in the nation's Capitol have even suggested a spiritistic version of the nuclear Manhattan Project (the government's all-out attempt to invent the atomic bomb) to explore clairvoyance, lest the Soviet Union get a step ahead in the field of occult adeptness.[2]

The precincts of the paranormal have been extended to nearly every respectable constituency of life. At the recent International Transpersonal Conference attended by nearly two thousand participants, most of them Ph.D. psychologists, I listened to a lecture on what used to be known as occult metaphysics. The talk was delivered by Dr. Russell Targ, a staff physicist with the Lockheed Research and Development Laboratories. This distinguished scientist compared academic investigation into the paranormal with the phenomena experienced 2,500 years ago by the oracles of Delphi.

With a bold face and without a blink, Dr. Targ discarded hundreds of years of scientific tradition by declaring, "Psychic function is a non-analytic ability. [It can't be objectively investigated because] analysis is the enemy of psychic functioning."[3]

The scientist also described his testing of well-known spiritualist medium Ingo Swan, who "could put his consciousness anywhere on the planet." Under the guise of objective research, Dr. Targ told of testing psychics who received mental images from photographs unseen by them but secretly selected by the examiners. The audience was shown slides of a crude line drawing made by a psychic who supposedly telepathically obtained the likeness of a monument from a picture of Grant's tomb. Dr. Targ also suggested that prophecy could be practiced by anyone. He unequivocally declared, "You can experience now the experience you will have an hour from now."[4]

The introduction to Satanism often comes from parapsychology. Not all casual investigators of the paranormal and New Age advocates are in league with the devil, but the arts they offer can open the mind to supernatural suggestions. Below is a brief description of PSI terms in case a teenager you know alludes to them.

PARAPSYCHOLOGY

By definition, parapsychology is that branch of the psychological sciences which deals with human faculties that are not operational within the limits of our five natural senses:

- *ESP* (extrasensory perception) is the catch-all category for such abilities.

• *Clairvoyance* refers to paranormal information received by touching an object or focusing mentally on an event.

• *Telepathy* is the awareness of the thoughts or the mental state of another person.

• *Cognition* is the knowledge of an event as it occurs. Knowing about something before it happens is called *precognition*. Awareness of an event after its occurrence is known as *postcognition*. Those possessing such abilities admit they lack control over the reception of this information.

• *Astral projection* (soul travel out of the body) is a practice highly touted by parapsychologists. Chad and Jamie had never attended an occult conference or read a parapsychological journal. Their knowledge of astral projection came from their absorption with society's familiarity with the paranormal, such as "Star Trek," an Arthur C. Clarke novel, a horror flick, or a grocery store tabloid.

It would be hard for any parent or counselor to pin down where curious children get ideas about the occult because our culture is saturated with notions about the supernatural. The pervasiveness of occult information that snared Chad and Jamie is the nemesis of parents who want to keep their children from such unsavory affiliations.

SATAN'S PSI IN THE NEW AGE

Plyers of the paranormal are no longer turbaned gurus gazing into smokey crystal balls. They don't claim to accurately predict the future or tell fortunes. Their New Age outlook peers more directly into the soul. America is their metaphysical mecca. Rebirthers, numerologists, mind control metaphysicians, crystal experts, trance channelers, and bodywork authorities abound. In the opinion of one college professor who has studied the historical origins of the New Age Movement, "It's really good old-fashioned occultism and superstition gussied up with pseudo-scientific jargon to give it an air of legitimacy."[5]

How does this cultural milieu of occultism affect the teenager introduced to Satanism? A subtle shift in societal attitudes has been occurring over the last decade. The New Age Movement and other popular mystical legacies have indoctrinated a generation to be-lieve that self-preoccupation is an appropriate goal. Religious tradi-tions based on Eastern modes of thought have gradually negated the Judeo-Christian concept of the conscience. Few youth today worry about the moral consequences of their actions.

This shift in cultural consciousness has removed an intangible inner barrier that guards against the occult. In prior generations, those who professed no religious faith were wary about demons and devils. They may not have believed in spiritualism, but they didn't mess with it, either. Today's teens, raised on the influence of "Friday the 13th"'s Jason and "Nightmare"'s Freddy Krueger, aren't awed by evil. If Nancy Reagan does it, if our nation's elected leaders do it, and if soft-spoken talk show guests do it, why not me? Thus, a fearsome door to the supernatural opens ever so casually, with no idea about who or what stands on the other side.

TRANCE CHANNELING

Until recently, seances were shadowy, even shady affairs. Seek-ers of the supernatural circled a table with their hands placed lightly on its top, lowered the lights, and awaited signs of a spirit's presence. A flickering candle, a whoosh of wind, a slight tip of the table, or a wispy voice was enough to guarantee success. In some cases, a trumpet-shaped device appeared, and a voice was heard from the void. On rare occasions, an apparition manifested itself as a departed loved one or famous personage.

Shirley MacLaine and other New Age proponents have refined the process and upped the ante on the entities. Darkened drawing rooms are unnecessary. Higher consciousness seminars offer trance-channelled messages under the glare of kleig lamps. The entire affair is videotaped in hotel ballrooms. Visitations of de-parted aunts and expired grandparents are too trivial. Present day channelers are human radios, allowing the masses to tune in ad-vanced spiritual information without an arduous search through sacred scriptures and ascetic disciplines.

Communication with discarnate entities has become a big pas-time and big business, from attempts to speak with Elvis to trance-channeled New Age ascended masters. Channeler J. Z. Knight claims to summon Ramtha, a thirty-five-thousand-year-old entity from the lost continent of Atlantis. For a seminar attendance fee of four hundred dollars, searching souls learn that California will sink into the ocean and acid rain will pollute New England's water supply. Kevin Ryerson, the channeler who tutored Shirley MacLaine on her New Age Quest for transcendent reality, claims 75 percent accuracy for the information his discarnate entity dispenses. Others, who are unwilling to contact the intangible through an intermediary, beckon us to become involved in their direct communication with the dead.

Teenagers are following adults in this search for psychic communication. Consider the case of a teenage friend of Satanist murderer, Ricky Kasso. While Kasso was being drawn deep into the dark, diabolical realms of manslaughter, his friend conducted seances to call forth the Prince of Darkness. The teen etched a five-pointed star on a table, placed a cup in the center, and put cigarette butts and a piece of paper in it. The participants chanted, "Satan will come forth in the form of fire." Suddenly, the cigarettes and paper burst into flames. "Welcome! Satan has arrived," the youth exulted.[6] Unfortunately for his victim, Ricky Kasso's conjuration of depraved demons was more than a puff of smoke.

HALLOWEEN HIGH JINKS

For parents of younger children, one additional aspect of the occult's cultural invasion must be addressed: Halloween. Don't assume this holiday is irrelevant to Satanism. You may be surprised at the way October 31 has become a prologue to our acceptance of the occult. Believe it or not, Halloween has become the devil's day, ritualistically recognized by some devil worshipers and occult groups throughout the nation.

What are the facts about Halloween? Is it a time to invoke the ancient Cornish prayer, "From ghoulies and ghosties and long leggety beasties and things that go bump in the night, good Lord deliver us"? Let's take a brief look at the history of this holiday.

THE DEVIL'S DAY

The Christian predecessor of Halloween, the Roman Catholic Church's All Saints Day, was originally celebrated in May, not November 1. In A.D. 608 the Roman emperor Constantine appeased the populace of newly conquered heathen territories by allowing them to combine their ancient ritual of Samhain Day with the newly-dated All Saints Day. Rome's pantheon, a temple built to worship a multiplicity of gods, was converted into a church. While Christians celebrated the death of departed saints, pagans devoted the preceding night to their Lord of the Dead.

The Witches' Sabbat

The choosing of the date of October 31 is no coincidence. October 31 is one of four major witches' sabbats, the four "cross-quarter" days of the Celtic calendar. The first, February 2, commonly known as Ground-Hog Day, honored Brigit, the pagan goddess of healing. The second, a May holiday called Beltane, was witchcraft's time to plant. On this day the druids performed magical rites to encourage the growth of crops. The third, an August harvest festival in honor of the sun god, commemorated the shining one, Lugh. These first three cross-quarter days marked the passing of seasons, the time to plant, and the time to harvest, as well as the time of the earth's death and rebirth. The last, Samhain, marked the coming of winter. At this time, the ancient druids performed rituals in which a cauldron symbolized the abundance of the goddess. It was said to be a time of "betwixt and between," a sacred season of superstition and spirit conjurations.

To the druids, October 31 was the night Samhain returned with the spirits of the dead. They had to be appeased or "treated" or the living would be tricked. Huge bonfires were set on hilltops to frighten away evil spirits and placate supernatural powers that controlled the processes of nature. More recently, European immigrants, particularly the Irish, introduced Halloween to America. By the late nineteenth century, its customs had become popular. It was an occasion to overturn outhouses, inflict property damage, and indulge in deviltry that wouldn't be tolerated at other times of the year.

Today, Halloween is a banner day for merchants. It's a night when decent people become outrageous exhibitionists. Sixty percent of all Halloween costumes are sold to adults. On October 31, one of every four people between the ages of eighteen and forty will dress up as some kind of character.[7] For psychic readers, clairvoyants, and self-proclaimed visionaries, it's the busiest time of the year. Publishers of books on subjects ranging from astrology to witchcraft indicate a dramatic increase in sales. Salem, Massachusetts, home of American witchcraft, now celebrates a "haunted happening" at Halloween to expand its summer tourist season.

HALLOWEEN'S SYMBOLS OF SATAN

The traditional practices associated with Halloween are easily identified with the occult. The jack o' lantern came from the tale of a notorious man named Jack, who was turned away from both heaven and hell. Consigned to roam the earth as a spirit, Jack put a glowing coal into a carved-out turnip to light his way through the night. This harbinger (which became a pumpkin) symbolized a damned soul. The colors orange and black can also be traced to the occult. They were connected with commemorative masses for the dead which were held in November. The unbleached beeswax candles used in the ceremony were orange, and the ceremonial caskets were covered by black cloths.

Other obvious ties Halloween has with the occult are:

• Halloween costumes are taken from the Celtic druid idea that ceremonial participants should wear animal heads and animal skins to acquire the strength of the beast they portrayed.

• Trick or treat came from the Irish tradition when a man led a procession to levy contributions from farmers, lest their crops be cursed by demons.

• Dunking for apples came from the old practice of divining the future. The participant who successfully clenched an apple between his teeth could count on a fulfilling romance with the lover of his choice.

• Cats represented incarnated humans, malevolent spirits, or the "familiars" of witches.

• Hazel nuts were used in romance divination. Some Halloween food had objects placed inside as a means of fortunetelling.

• Masks have traditionally been an animistic means of superstitiously warding off evil spirits or changing the personality of the wearer to communicate with the spirit world.

Halloween has other negative aspects besides a pagan background rooted in witchcraft and its emphasis on the devil and darkness. Some vandals are more interested in playing tricks than getting treats. Parents worry that a demented criminal will distribute poisoned candy or goodies containing pins and razor blades. There's also the danger that motorists won't see costumed kids walking on dark streets.

Such evil associations do not suggest that a parent permitting Halloween celebrations is in collaboration with the devil. But you would be hard pressed to think of one positive virtue in Halloween. Its symbolism involves demons, ghosts, death, darkness, skeletons, fear, and terror.

CHRISTIANS CONFRONTING HALLOWEEN

Some anti-occult groups have successfully removed Halloween celebrations from public schools. Recently, an Arkansas minister filed a federal court suit, demanding that Satanism-via-Halloween observances should not be tolerated in schools while prayer is banned. The Reverend Ralph Forbes named the devil as the defendant.

One mother, who led a similar fight to remove Halloween from the public schools, said she didn't mind the day being observed as a fall festival with children dressing up as characters from American history, but she drew the line at accenting the holiday's shadowy side. In her words, "If the principle of sectarianism has taken Christmas celebrations out of the schools, why not Halloween? If they can't honor God, why honor the devil?"

Opponents of such attempts to censor Halloween say that it is not a religious celebration and that anti-Halloween advocates are curmudgeons whose overactive imaginations spoil children's fun. Is a more serious appraisal concerning the eve of All Hallows (Saints) Day overdue? Ask the Chicago shelter for stray cats. Each Halloween, they report that inquiries about black cats increase. Fearing that the felines are being used in bloody rituals by self-proclaimed witches, the Anti-Cruelty Society has made black cats off limits for adoption during the Halloween season.

All this has witches wondering. Leo Louis Martello, high priest of a witchcraft coven and author of a book about the craft, entitled

The Old Time Religion, is the director of the Witches' Anti-Defamation League. He says, "True witchcraft has been a persecuted minority religion. They are now coming out of their broom closets and fighting back."[8] *USA Today* joined the fracas by declaring, "No rational person looks at Halloween as a celebration of Satanism."[9]

In this contemporary world of all-too-real satanic evil, many think it is time to cleanse Halloween of its unsavory elements. They feel a ban on official observances of Halloween would warn parents and children that Halloween's occult symbology celebrates dark and dangerous spiritual powers. At least parents could center family activities around wholesome fun. They could have a party, but condemn costumes that relate to evil. For instance, some churches celebrate All Saints Day by having children dress as saints of the Bible. Children are never too young to learn that a day should not be dedicated to the devil.

THE SLIPPERY SIDE OF SATANISM

Like so many in our culture, Chad and Jamie were guileless victims of Satanism. They weren't looking for evil, but wickedness lurked behind the reflections they saw in the mirror.

"If the devil wanted to destroy your soul, could you say 'No'?" I asked Chad.

"Yes," he said.

"Then consider this. If you go through the mirror, you're gone. Get it? You aren't there to protect your soul," I pointed out.

Suddenly Chad understood. In the course of our conversation, he concluded that Satan is tricky, the occult is dangerous, and failing to provide a sentry for the soul can be spiritually disastrous.

Chad had been listening to "TALK-BACK" for four days. Earlier the day he called, he had told Jamie to listen that afternoon. Jamie had promised to do so, yet minutes before the show started he fell asleep.

In the middle of my conversation with Chad that day, Jamie was abruptly awakened by his barking dog. He turned on the radio, heard me talking with Chad, and rushed to Chad's house to join the conversation. He, too, decided to be leery of Satanism.

Was the barking dog a coincidence? Perhaps. But also consider how Chad had originally heard me on the radio.

"I shared my occult encounters with our mailman," he told me.

"Tune in to 'TALK-BACK with Bob Larson," the U.S. Postal Service employee advised Chad.

Such coincidences—some would say divine intervention—give me hope that Satan cannot triumph totally.

Seances, frightful films, occult experimentation, sinister songs— these contemporary corruptions are luring many souls deep into demonic darkness. In the midst of such negativism, God promises those who sincerely seek truth and love that the power of good is greater than the essence of evil.[10] For the parent who worries about raising a child in the midst of a satanic society, there is hope. Evil abounds, but so do helpful mailmen and barking dogs.

THE TEENAGE SEARCH FOR TRUTH

One benefit of the current interest in the occult and parapsychology is the teenage search for truth and spiritual meaning. On "TALK-BACK" we recently conducted a three-month series on teen problems. Topics ranged from drugs to runaways, gangs to suicide. Although normally we have our smallest listening audience during June, July, and August, this series broke all records for response. Teenagers bombarded our on-the-air lines with fiercely frank questions and comments about life, God, and the devil.

"Why did you call?" I asked often.

"Nobody pays any attention to me. I just wanted someone to talk to" was the common response.

"Does anyone love you?" I queried several times.

"No one. Not even my parents" was the usual answer.

In fact, during the entire three months, not a single teenager unhesitatingly confirmed he was assured of parental love.

One of the teen topic callers, David, the Slayer fan in Chapter 1, answered the question, "Who loves you?" this way:

"Nobody. I love myself. That's all."

"What about your mother?"

"Nah, I don't think so."

"Your father?"

"I doubt it."

"What are your parents like?"

"I don't know. They don't talk to me any more."

"David, I care about you. That's why I'm taking so much time to talk to you. What worries me is that before you find out people care about you, Satan will convince you to kill yourself," I warned David.

"That's the price I'll have to pay," he glibly answered.

Earlier in our conversation, I had asked David, "Why are you so angry?"

"This world has no love," David responded. "Hate is better than love. I can see the effects of hatred and what it does to people. I can't see love."

"Hate hasn't won yet," I countered.

"You're wrong! Hate always wins," David argued.

"Hate may be winning temporarily in your life, but it doesn't win in the world. Hate loses every time a new baby is born. Hate is defeated each time a doctor performs an operation and restores someone's life."

David kept coming back at me. "Hate wins when a psychopathic killer murders people. Even when a kid is born, he dies after eighty years."

"Hate loses every time a Mother Theresa reaches out to comfort the dying," I retorted.

"Personally, I think the whole world deserves to die!" David exclaimed. "You don't deserve to live. I'm not going to kill you, but you should kill yourself. Satanists who worship my god are the only ones who deserve to live."

Teens today are struggling with the issue of good and evil, just as David was. During that three-month series on youth problems, teenagers asked about hell, demons, trance channelling, visions, dreams, ESP, necromancy—almost every aspect of the occult. If God is there, they wanted to know, "Why does evil abound?" If Satan exists, they wondered, "Is his promise of power in exchange for allegiance a deceptive tactic or a legitimate offer?"

Since today's teens are deeply interested in subjects of spiritual significance, parents should ask themselves:

- Have I ever talked to my child about God and the existence of evil in the world?
- Have I ever explained the supernatural to my child and discussed the presence of Satanism in our society?
- Am I involved in parapsychology or New Age philosophy which would indicate my acceptance of the occult?
- Do we have the kind of forthright communication in our family that allows for an easy exchange of ideas across the generation gap?
- If someone asked my child, "Does anyone love you?," what would he answer?

Chad's and Jamie's encounter with evil occurred so casually that parents should see how easily their children can become involved in the occult. Kids must know their parents love them unconditionally. If they wander into evil ways, they must be able to depend on their parents to respond quickly with alarm and concern.

If your child embraces the paranormal, as Chad and Jamie did, quickly warn him that the idea of possessing boundless untapped powers of the soul is as old as Eden.[11] Admonish him against assuming such forces are a kind of biocosmic energy, like The Force of "Star Wars." It doesn't matter whether psychic abilities come from the soul or Satan. Their lure of pride and power is self-destructive, occult enticements into more threatening facets of the slippery side of Satanism.

4

Ghoulish Games

"My character is a priest. He uses supernatural powers just like the magic users do. But his alignment is lawful good, so there's nothing wrong with it," Robert argued. "I called your radio show today to set you straight. It's a game of fantasy. Playing Dungeons & Dragons (D&D) doesn't certify you as a witch."

Robert wasn't through leveling his salvo. "Dungeons & Dragons is one of the cleanest, funnest, and most mentally challenging games you could play," he insisted.

Robert is typical of Dungeons & Dragons players. His interest in fantasy role-playing games is fueled by an inquisitive intellect often left unchallenged by routine rigors of schoolwork. He escapes into a fictional realm by becoming absorbed in a fabricated world of medieval imagery, where his mind conjures heroics and adventure at whim.

"Isn't it dangerous to fool around with occult realities, even in an illusory fashion?" I countered.

"No," Robert said. "It's a test of your acting and imagination."

"But your character, the priest, uses occult forces."

"It's fantasy power," Robert responded. "There's nothing real in D&D."

Before you accept Robert's rebuttal, let's look carefully at Dungeons & Dragons (D&D) and other ghoulish games.

Kids like Chad and Jamie, who played "Bloody Mary" in their spare time, don't get involved in evil overnight. Many young people first encounter the occult in their homes as they crouch over game boards that answer questions or predict behavior.

Games based on occult powers and principles are seldom taken seriously, but they do presume that consulting unseen forces is child's play. The teens who call my talk show seeking help often mention Dungeons & Dragons and other occult games as their introduction to Satanism.

THE LURE OF DUNGEONS & DRAGONS

Numerous case studies indicate that Dungeons & Dragons results in dangerous consequences. In the following criminal cases, the youngsters were all obsessed with Dungeons & Dragons, and critics blamed the game's influence for their violations:

- In California, the body of a bright seventeen-year-old boy washed up on a San Francisco beach.
- In Colorado, a twelve-year-old lad fatally shot his sixteen-year-old brother, then killed himself.
- In Kansas, a fourteen-year-old Eagle Scout candidate walked into his junior high school and opened fire with a rifle, killing his principal and three others.
- In Austin, Texas, a twelve-year-old boy jumped to his death from a hotel window.

The National Coalition on Television Violence says D&D is linked to more than fifty teenage deaths. One attorney, representing the family of a young suicide victim who was involved in D&D, declared, "It is a game that tells kids how to perfect the art of premeditated murder."[1]

THE STRATEGY OF D&D

Dungeons & Dragons began as a spin-off of war games. Gary Gygax, D&D's inventor, discarded familiar game components like cards, boards, and six-sided dice, and devised a game with no rules or time limits. A single game of D&D can last for hours, days, weeks, months, or even years. At least three people must play. One is the Dungeon Master, a controlling figure who devises the dungeon map and directs the game's flow. The other players are pitted against each other. They roll poly-sided dice to determine the various intelligence and dexterity ratings of their alter-ego characters, which are given fictitious names.

The players gather around a fictitious or roughly sketched map and set off on an imaginary odyssey through hazardous terrain created by the Dungeon Master. En route, they encounter obstacles, such as monsters and demons, which they thwart with violent tactics and occult spells. No one wins. The object is to survive the adventure and participate in the next game with an even more powerful character.

In my telephone conversation with Robert, the teenager who called "TALK-BACK" to defend D&D, I asked, "Isn't success in the game based on using treachery and violence?"

"Yes. In fact, my character got angry once and messed up some people. In my imagination he physically beat them up."

"How can you defend your character, a Christian priest, taking violent, revengeful action?"

Robert was cornered, and he responded protectively. "Christians aren't perfect. Anyway, the bad background of D&D is what makes it interesting. It shouldn't be played in church. It's OK, if you don't take it seriously."

The use of murder, arson, torture, rape, robbery, and the occult to endure the quest for the dungeon may not concern teens like Robert, but it does distress some. One former player admitted, "I derived a sadistic sort of pleasure from killing evil people in the game. If an evil character threatened me, I'd subconsciously treat him just like one of those junior high jokers who put me down. I was using D&D instead of the real world to work out my problems. In my D&D world, I had the power to alter events."[2]

SATANISM'S LINK WITH D&D

Some aspects of D&D are directly linked with Satanism. The extent of occult collusion depends partly on the manuals selected to guide the game and formulate the dungeon master's strategy. Some manuals tell players how to summon demons and indulge in astral projection. At minimum, D&D replaces reality with a contrived universe where anything goes and moral absolutism is absent. Certain players may become so detached from the outside world that the death of their character triggers violent rage.

It is obvious that writers for the various manuals associated with fantasy role-playing games are well-versed in the occult. Pentagrams and potions are frequently recommended. In the manual *Deities and Demigods,* the writer advises, "Serving a deity is a significant part of D&D, and all player characters should have a patron god."

Isaac Bonewits, a well-known practicing witch, considers Dungeons & Dragons such a good instructional mechanism to paganism that he has written a book showing players how to move from D&D into real sorcery. His special manual on demons describes the appearance and power of evil entities with accompanying sketches.

The Official Advanced D&D Handbook

The *Official Advanced Dungeons & Dragons Players Handbook,* written by game founder Gygax and published by the game manufacturer, TSR, Inc., is an explicit education in occultism. Gygax wastes no time, informing his protégés, "The casting of spells, clerical and magical, is a very important aspect of play. Most spells have a *verbal* component, and so must be uttered. . . . Clerical spells, including the druidic [witchcraft], are bestowed by gods so that the desired . . . spell components will be placed properly in his or her mind." Gygax continues instructing players to memorize the appropriate spells to "impress the potent, mystical spell formulae upon the mind."[3]

Dungeons & Dragons' clerical spells are recited as bewitching chants. An opposing character may be dispatched by what is called a "necromantic Slow Poison." A "Spiritual Hammer" may be used to create a force field, striking any adversary in sight. The player may use divination spells to acquire "information regarding the relative strength of creatures in the area . . . and the relative chances for incurring the wrath of evil or good supernatural." Clerics can also perform "resurrections," bringing back to life imaginary characters that have been dead up to ten years.[4]

The Official Advanced Legends and Lore Manual

The official *Legends and Lore* manual explicitly describes a pantheon of pagan deities taken from the mythology of native American Indian spirits, Babylonian gods, Celtic [witchcraft] deities, and Egyptian divinities. The manual warns, "The mighty evil gods, demons, and devils are prone to appear when their name is spoken . . ."[5]

Even out-of-the-body experiences are discussed. *Legends and Lore* explains, "When deities and their minions travel to planes other than their own, they are mystically anchored to their home plane by a metaphysical 'silver cord': this is similar to the one described for *astral spell* . . ."[6]

The specific instructions given to D&D players regarding demons and deities are alarming. Seekers of Indian spirits are told to dress their character in occult symbols to summon the serpents of the Snakeman. Those who evoke the Babylonian god Durga are warned he may "occasionally send a group of devils out to aid his worshipers, especially those that have recently sacrificed a virgin to their deity."[7]

The occult overtones of D&D are so explicit that virtually nothing in the world of Satanism is omitted. Players are told how to have their characters commune with nature spirits, consult crystal balls filled with human blood, and conjure the Egyptian deities that Moses opposed (Set, Ra, Isis, Osiris, Horus, Bes). Most disturbing are precise directions regarding Celtic human sacrifices. The place and manner of performing such sacrifices is detailed, along with the calendar dates for the appropriate high unholy days (including November 1, Samhain, the Lord of the Dead, Lucifer, as explained in Chapter 3).[8]

Allegations of complicity with Satanism so alarmed defenders of Dungeons & Dragons that the Game Manufacturers Association published a pamphlet responding to the objections. The writer argued that "role-playing games no more make their players Satan worshipers than Monopoly makes its players slum landlords." Admitting D&D could be "a person's first exposure to the occult," and that some manuals contain information on Satanism, the pamphlet counters that no game "assumes a player will actually try to . . . call up a demon."[9] As for the idea that vicarious sin equals actual sin, the writer concludes such a concept is "farfetched," which is an unreserved denial of the teachings of Jesus Christ, who said that anyone looking lustfully has committed adultery in his heart.[10]

Most D&D players do not pursue its more evil aspects and argue they shouldn't be penalized for indulging in fantasy rather than actual evil. As one of my callers named Matt put it, "I only choose characters who represent biblical themes, and I never allow them to engage in immoral activities."

Another caller, Mike, claimed the contrary. "I decided as a Dungeon Master to create an imaginary universe based on Christian principles. Eventually, I had to abandon it. Dungeons & Dragons only succeeds effectively as a game if the players are allowed to use tactics of violence and the occult."

How can parents respond to the argument that D&D involves only imaginary evil? What should a teenager who is a Dungeons & Dragons player do the next time his character uses a spell?

Christian teaching underscores many objections to D&D, including the command to ignore evil imaginations and avoid "every thing that exalts itself against the knowledge of God, bringing every thought into captivity to the obedience of Christ."[11] This injunction accepts the fact that creative imagination is an important part of spirituality. How else could the creation of the world and the wonders of heaven, from Genesis to the Revelation, be comprehended?

In the world of D&D, no morality parallels that of the real world. There is no theistic accountability or intrusion of a Christian world view. Likewise, the motives of D&D characters indicate an exercise in expediency rather than moral perspective. The ancient writer of Proverbs warned, "For as he thinks in his heart, so is he."[12]

Not all D&D players are obsessive, but a constant compulsion to play the game is typical. Important time that could be spent on more fruitful activities is directed toward the inner world of the Dungeon Master. Robert, the young man who called defending D&D, admitted that he played nearly every day of the week, sometimes five or six hours a day. He's not alone. Many "TALK-BACK" callers confess playing the game even more frequently. No wonder Robert flinched at my suggestion that his pursuit was a perilous pastime.

The link with Satanism occurs when players use symbols and protective inscriptions associated with witchcraft and the occult. Necromancy (the biblically forbidden practice of communication with the dead) is sometimes used in D&D as a divinational means of deriving information. Such activity occurs in an imagined universe where the moral quality of the players' characters is often dichotomous.

One caller, Charles, explained that the roll of the dice gave him a character who was "neutral-good" with "chaotic-lawful" attributes.

"That's contradictory," I challenged Charles. "In reality, good is not neutral. The very idea of ethical neutrality supposes that our world exists in a moral vacuum.

"The idea of someone being chaotic-lawful is equally bogus," I went on. "Chaos by its nature causes anarchy. How could that be lawful?"

Charles gave the stock D&D answer: "Dungeons & Dragons is in your mind, and you can do anything you want mentally without actually doing evil."

That questionable logic aside, the truth is that Dungeons & Dragons guides participants into a world of nonmaterial entities, forces, and spirits. Obviously, if such beings exist, the line of demarcation between fantasy and reality can easily be blurred. Warn anyone you know who plays D&D, "There is no assurance that conjuring an imagined entity will prevent a real spirit from responding!"

Every addiction to the devil is preceded by mental and emotional addiction to evil. The mere discussion of occult evil in D&D manuals certainly doesn't condone exploring Satanism, but it is a *de facto* endorsement of the occult.

GAMES PEOPLE PLAY

Dungeons & Dragons isn't the only recreational diversion that links Satanism with game boards. Game, toy, and department stores are filled with dangerous divinatory devices that encourage supernatural experimentation. I will describe four games in this chapter. For additional information, consult the Appendix, where other ghoulish games are listed and described. The games mentioned in this chapter and Appendix A are only a few of the menacing occult diversions available in the marketplace.

A Nightmare on Elm Street

Based on the highly successful horror movie of the same name. Just as in the movie series where a victim killed in his dreams by Freddy Krueger dies in real life, players must move their pawns from the Nightmare side of the board to the Awake side and arouse from sleep before Freddy Krueger strikes. For the player who confronts the molesting murderer by the appearance of a Freddy Card, the only escape is to consign Mr. Finger-Knives to burn alive in the boiler room. Rhymes from the movie appear on matching cards, such as, "One, two, Freddy's coming for you. Three, four, better lock your door. Five, six, grab your crucifix."

Throughout the game, Freddy Krueger terrorizes and launches slaughtering sprees. He can move through walls, rise through the floor, and strike again after being killed. Game cards depict a frightened girl clutching a crucifix, a skeleton crawling across the floor, and Freddy holding a victim by the neck, ready to tear out the quarry's heart. Freddy portrays the embodiment of a supernatural evil being with mysterious strength. Nowhere is God or goodness called upon to triumph. Only by assault, violence, and terror (Freddy's tactics) can a successful player elude death and win.

Phenomenon

Designed for players ages twelve and older, Phenomenon encourages the exercise of telepathic, clairvoyant, extrasensory, and levitational power. Each player is given a Telepad to write down images received during the game. A fake plastic crystal is placed at the center of the board. Players move spaces determined by the die cast and choose an extrasensory exercise dependent on the color they land on. The idea is to tap into and experiment with extraordinary energies. Winning is achieved by believing that a psychic level can be attained by concentrating on unknown forces. An accompanying tape encourages a pre-game warm-up period when the players explore their creative, psychic selves.

In the extrasensory perception exercise, a player who lands on a diamond must go into the kitchen and sample specially prepared sweet, salty, sour, and spicy foods. Other players are receivers, who must use telepathic powers to guess which foods are being tasted. Players also test psychokinetic forces by attempting to move paper cups and levitate light objects, such as toothpicks. The player who wins is esteemed as one who is adept in paranormal power, a potential lure to deeper occult experimentation.

The Real Ghostbusters

Like games designed for younger players, The Real Ghostbusters is heavy on visuals and light on intrigue. The game board is accompanied by some minor construction involving an elaborate stairway, buildings, a knight with an axe, and a "ghost trap." The object is to collect four Ghost Cards and be the first to close the trap at the top of the stairs. Though a seemingly harmless game, it functions on the presumption that ghosts are "catchable."

Contact with the dead is assumed, as well as encounters with ghoulish goblins. Players roll a skull down the shaft when their turn ends on a Skull Space. Though the game's premise is pure fantasy, it implies that poltergeists are not to be taken seriously and supernatural manifestations are child's play. This idea is not overtly evil but meshes well with our culture's message that satanic realities are humorous and legendary, not authentic dangers.

Ouija Board

Parker Brothers, the game's manufacturer, is explicit about how to use this game. Players are admonished to take the endeavor seriously and not have a "frivolous spirit, asking ridiculous questions, laughing over it." The name ouija comes from the French word for yes, *oui,* and the German word for yes, *ja.* Many players can tell terrifying stories associated with Ouija's accurate answers.

The Ouija board is a piece of pressed cardboard with the numbers zero through nine, the letters of the alphabet, and the words *good, bye, yes,* and *no* printed on the surface. The teardrop-shaped plastic *planchette,* or counter, is placed on top. Two players face each other with the board on their laps. Participants' fingers rest lightly on the counter, allowing it to move freely over the board. Questions are posed, and the counter eventually moves. A hole in the counter's center stops over the selected letter, number, or word.

When a letter is chosen, consecutive movements of the counter choose additional letters to spell out words in response to the players' inquiry. Instructions declare, "It gives you entertainment you have never experienced. It draws the two people using it into a close relationship and weaves about them a feeling of mysterious isolation. It surpasses in its unique results mind reading, clairvoyance, and second sight. Loaded with fun, excitement, and thrills more intense and absorbingly interesting than a mystery story."

I've talked with hundreds of people who have played with Ouija.

Without exception, those who have asked the board to disclose its source of information have received the response: "demons, devils, Satan, Beelzebub, Lucifer," or a satanic equivalent. Either unconscious assumptions were made by the players, triggering muscular responses to the question, or the reply was truthful. If the latter, the Ouija board is a spiritually dangerous tool of evil invasion.

THE OCCULT DOOR OF DIVINATION

The connection to witchcraft and Satanism is even more obvious with occult means of divination. These are not games but serious attempts to know the unknown and control capricious forces underlying the material universe. The I Ching, Tarot cards, palmistry, tea leaf reading, fortunetelling, astrology, and the prophecies of Nostradamus are gateways to the world of occultism. Though socially popular, these mechanisms introduce subjective, non-rational interpretations of reality. Abrogation of the mind and reasoning powers often leads to acceptance of mystical explanations of reality. Once the door is opened, evil may enter in masquerade.

The majority who consult horoscopes or confer with Tarot card readers never entertain darker desires. But basing one's life on non-cognitive directives can lead to other arcane, less innocuous interests. Those who respect the Scriptures can hardly avoid the warning God gave the Israelites against such practices: "There shall not be found among you *anyone* who . . . practices witchcraft, or a soothsayer, or one who interprets omens, or a sorcerer, or one who conjures spells, or a medium, or a spiritist, or one who calls up the dead. For all who do these things are an abomination to the Lord . . ."[13]

Many who probe forms of ancient occultism adhere to the dictum of Carl Jung, Freud's associate, who said, "Anything that has been around that long has to have truth to it." Consequently, the I Ching, which is said to have existed in China as early as 3000 B.C., must have some prognosticative value. In our highly restrictive world of defined roles and goals, the idea of knowledge beyond logical laws is enticing. Thus, the occult becomes an escape route from the drabness of everyday drudgery.

Instead of turning outward to science and the arts, the occult practitioner looks inward to plumb subliminal depths. This retreat from reality creates an occult fiction motivated by the magical and symbolical. After months or years of such absorption, almost anyone is ripe for outlandish possibilities, including the blatant worship of evil.

I Ching

The I Ching, *Book of Changes*, is an ancient Chinese volume of collective wisdom. It is consulted in conjunction with the casting of yarrow sticks or the tossing of coins. The lay of the sticks or coins forms patterns which are said to reveal unconscious tendencies that the I Ching glyphs and hexagrams interpret spiritually and psychologically.

Tarot Cards

The seventy-eight cards of the Tarot deck are of undetermined origin. Some say the eighteenth-century French philologist, Count de Gebelin, originated the suits, though other occultists claim an earlier origin in the ancient Egyptian *Book of Thoth*. Each card's symbolic form supposedly has several possible intuitive interpretations, depending on the reader.

Palmistry

Palmistry suggests that the lines of one's open hand reveal events connected with inherent emotional qualities. The color and texture of skin, along with the direction and length of each line, supposedly reveal the inner secrets of health and longevity.

Tea Leaves

Tea-leaf reading surveys the lay of leaves in the bottom of an emptied cup. Occult lore holds that the bowl of the cup corresponds to the dome of the sky and the leaves are like stars in conjunctive configurations.

Astrology

Astrology adheres to the concept that one's predictive qualities are determined by the relative positions of heavenly bodies at the moment of birth. The planets, phases of the moon, and stellar positions are all factored to determine one's sign and characteristics. Though universally rejected by scientists and astronomers, astrology is popular in this uncertain era. If institutions and traditions are no longer reliable, astrologers claim that the unchanging location of heavenly bodies imprints each life with a plan that astrologers can discern.

Nostradamus

The poetic prophecies of the sixteenth-century French occultist, Nostradamus, are an increasingly fashionable form of divination. His book, *The Centuries,* consists of a hundred verses composed in quatrains. His colorful and highly metaphorical language has resulted in a variety of translations. Nostradamus' oblique writings have been credited with predicting the assassination of the Kennedys and the rise of Hitler. Some thought the French word "hister" in one of Nostradamus' quatrains was an anagram for Hitler.

Involvement in occultism encourages an introspective individualization process. The emotionally dysfunctional will become more self-absorbed and less likely to deal realistically with life's problems. This is especially problematic with youth. A teenager is at a crucial developmental stage in life when the cultivation of relationships is vital. When the young person turns inward, to be guided by intuitive discovery, he shuts off eternal emotive mechanisms, creating an artificial realm directed by inner urges. This curtails the outside world of psychological checks and balances, which can be spiritually devastating. I pointed this out to Robert, the Dungeons & Dragon player whose story started this chapter.

ROBERT'S REBUTTAL

"Because your D&D character is an emotional extension of you," I told Robert, "making such an investment of yourself is psychologically dangerous.

"You're creating an alter-ego," I explained. "There is a danger that you and your character will fuse emotionally. When that happens, the occult traits and the violent tendencies of your character will become part of you."

Robert didn't yield. He insisted the challenge to his mind was worth the risk.

"Pornography is also emotionally challenging," I argued. "But that kind of fantasy is equally wrong. Evil exists, and the line between illusion and reality can be too easily passed over."

My showdown with Robert didn't stop him from playing D&D. I had no authority to insist that he quit. A parent's position is different. If your child plays Dungeons & Dragons, a confrontation may be necessary. The potential for evil associations is so great that even a casual interest in D&D shouldn't be taken lightly.

But before you can alert your child to the harm of D&D, you must first establish a mutually loving relationship. Your child must know that you are approaching him in an informed and genuinely concerned manner.

"That's not going to be easy," you say.

Certainly not. So, let me pass on some lessons I've learned from hundreds of calls to "TALK-BACK." My advice isn't foolproof, but these simple instructions will help you activate the power of communication.

First, know what you're talking about. Nothing turns off a teen quicker than an uninformed inquiry. My youthful callers listen to me because I've taken the time to learn about their world. In the case of occult games or devices, do some investigating. Then approach your child from an apprised perspective. If you don't understand something, don't be afraid to ask. "What do you mean by that?" I often ask. Accept their answers uncritically. Generally, teenagers are eager to let you enter their private domain if they sense you are not judgmental.

Second, let your child know it's the forest, not the trees, that concerns you. Try my technique of asking questions to get the big picture. Usually, curiosity about the occult implies that a child's practical, spiritual, and emotional needs are not being met.

"What's really bothering you down inside?" I may ask, probing gently. Occult fascination is the branch. Get to the root. Many children abandon spiritual faith because they see their parents' religion as sterile and ineffectual. Be prepared to examine your own life.

Third, be tough, but treat your teen respectfully. "That's garbage," I may say, bluntly putting it to a teen. "You don't mean that. Get serious with me, and say what's really on your mind." But once I pressure him to talk about his predicament, I back off and give him a chance to converse at his own pace. The art of listening has been lost by too many parents.

Finally, let your child know he can say what's on his mind without fear of retribution. Teenagers tell me incredible things because they know I won't recoil with shock or tell them not to express themselves so provocatively. Be prepared for shock! Kids today use frank language and aren't afraid to verbally lay it on the line. Don't worry about your sensibilities. Such apprehension stifles communication with youth.

Above all, start talking. You may feel inadequate at first. You may be overcome with thoughts of desperation and incompetence. You may fear rejection from your child. But keep talking to him, and keep loving him. It won't be an easy task. But when Satan wants your child, the stakes are immeasurable and eternal.

5

Nightmare on Main Street

"What's so bad about horror films like 'Nightmare on Elm Street?' It wasn't until the latest episode that Freddy Krueger actually killed someone in real life. Before it was always in someone's dream."

Jerry, a young man in his early twenties, dialed the day the "TALK-BACK" topic was "Horror Films." He began the conversation by defending slice-and-dice flicks. As the dialogue progressed, he admitted such movies affected him.

"'Nightmare on Elm Street' isn't the worst horror movie," Jerry argued. "My favorite is 'Hotel Hell,' although it did make me barf up my popcorn. Some guy chops people up and makes fritters out of them.

"I don't know about other people, but these films make me want to act out what I've seen," Jerry conceded. "I used to come home and try weird things out on my wife."

"Like what?" I asked.

"The worst was the time I saw a Vincent Price film. Some guy discovered another guy didn't like him. So he found some dogs, killed them, and made pudding out of them."

"Dog pudding? You've got to be kidding.'"

"No. He made the other guy eat it."

"What's that got to do with your wife?"

"When I got home from seeing the movie, I got drunk and killed the family dog."

"Oh, no! . . . Let me guess. You made your wife eat it?"

"She didn't know what it was. I told her it was a special new recipe I made just for her."

I was grateful Jerry hadn't done anything worse. If he had really wanted to imitate horror film "art," his conduct could have been even more depraved.

THE HORROR OF HORROR MOVIES

Gross-out movies are big grossers on the screen and on video. Zombies, mutants, deranged murderers, and psychological torturers wreak wholesale havoc on a scale the gore industry calls KPMs—killings per minute. In today's horror genre, children possess psychic abilities to start fires at will. Nightmarish dreams turn into reality. Mutilated denizens of the deep crawl out of human flesh. Even automobiles come alive with demonic design, as Stephen King's deadly 1958 red Plymouth, Christine, illustrated in the movie of the same name.

This film trend started in 1974 with the horror classic, "The Texas Chain Saw Massacre," the story of five unsuspecting teenagers who became the main course for a family of homicidal cannibals. Today an ad for the video "Demons" reads, "This movie grabs you by the throat and stomps the life out of you. These are demons of death, vicious, bloodthirsty creatures who step from the screen into your lap. The worst part is, there's no way out. Unless, of course, you consider death a reasonable alternative."

Currently, horror movies make up 18.2 percent of available video software.[1] Often a movie that bombs at the box office becomes a hit at home. "Creepers," which brought in less than a million dollars in the theaters, earned $3.3 million in video cassette sales with a $79.95 list price. Independent TV stations have launched a campaign of blood, sweat, and fear by airing blocks of scary syndicated shows on weekend nights. Critics call it "splatter" television, referring to all the blood spilled in living color. One horror star commented on TV gore, "We're getting away with murder."[2]

Who watches such fare? While researching the phenomenon of horror films, I assumed the unpleasant duty of sitting through hours of ritualized, satanic, screen savagery. Most of these movies were R-rated. Yet almost always I was the oldest person and only adult in the theater. Average age? Approximately fifteen. The worst part was audience reaction as bodies were disemboweled and limbs amputated. Instead of hung heads and disapproving groans, the murderous mayhem met with cheers, laughter, and indifference.

"Chop his head off!" someone in the audience yelled, as the movie portrayed a frightened, ax-wielding teenager turning on her tormentor.

A decapitated head dropped to the floor. "Slice him again!" another movie fan hollered in encouragement.

While blood streamed across the screen and a disemboweled body writhed in agony, a six-year-old in the audience nonchalantly asked his sister, "Get me some more popcorn?"

"Wow! That looked real," a teenager said to his friend, as the spiny fingers of an armless hand ripped out a victim's eyeballs.

Blood, guts, and gore on the screen. Popcorn, candy, and pop for the audience. No one gagged or grimaced. Beyond shock, the kids intently observed the wizardry of special effects that simulated savagery.

Since you weren't in the theaters to see for yourself, come with me on a spine-tingling journey through the world of horror films to consider their effect.

AN UNLUCKY FRIDAY THE 13TH

The "Friday the 13th" tetralogy is based on the character Jason, whose mother went on a vengeful killing spree in the first movie in the series. After his murderous mom was killed, Jason took over with a gusto that would do a psychopath proud, dispatching campers, vacationers, and anyone else who got in his way. The reward for such savagery? "Final Chapter," the fourth in the violent "Friday the 13th" film series, grossed $11.2 million the first weekend it opened.

The outcome for others? Ask the parents of Sharon Gregory of Greenfield, Massachusetts. Mark Branch, a nineteen-year-old horror movie fan, killed their teenage daughter. The young woman, who was acquainted with Branch, was found in her bathtub. She had been stabbed repeatedly.

Branch had frequently rented horror films from local video stores, and police later found horror movie memorabilia at his home. Among the things they came across were video cassettes of "Friday the 13th" and a hockey mask—trademark of Jason, the movie's slasher. Police reported that Branch was so obsessed with Jason he "wanted to see what it feels like to kill."[3]

What fascinated Branch? In "Friday the 13th, the Final Chapter," a carefree teenage boy searches a kitchen for a corkscrew. Suddenly the elusive utensil, wielded by an unseen assailant, flashes out of nowhere and impales his hand against the countertop. Then an ax cleaves his skull between the eyes. Unfortunately, the "Final Chapter" wasn't final. "Friday the 13th—A New Beginning" followed, featuring more than twenty killings.

The outcome for Branch? Police later found his dead body hanging from a limb in the woods near Buckland, Massachusetts.

ONE, TWO, THREE, FOUR, BETTER LOCK YOUR FAMILY'S DOOR

No horror series has been more successful than the "Nightmare on Elm Street" sagas, starring incinerated child molester Freddy Krueger. In the original 1984 version, Krueger was a janitor at a small-town high school. After murdering innocent adolescents, Freddy was burned in the school furnace. Like "Friday the 13th"'s Jason, Freddy is dispatched at the end of each episode, only to return again, again, and again, his finger-knives poised to disembowel and decapitate.

Each time Freddy returns, he appears in dreams. But if Freddy kills you nocturnally, you're dead for real. Ironically, Freddy's rubbery, disfigured face, his glove with five-inch knife blades, and his tormenting terror constitute a *de rigueur* adolescent ceremony of Satanism. Teenagers can unanimously cite Freddy's liturgy of atrocity: "One, two, I'm coming for you. Three, four, better lock your door."

No one anticipated that this grade Z horror movie would turn into a cottage industry. The original version cost $1.8 million to make and earned $24 million. The first three installments of "Night-mare" brought in $103 million. Sales of ancillary merchandise have topped $15 million. Freddy's mask outsells all others at Halloween, and record albums, two "Nightmare" books, a board game, and Freddy dolls honor this suburban psychopath.

Condemning the criminal influence of horror films is made diffi-cult by one simple fact. The perpetrators of emulated violence aren't around to confess. Mark Branch killed himself and can't tell us what motivated him. The same is true of Sean Helms. On Janu-ary 28, 1987, the eighteen-year-old of Indianapolis, Indiana, was playing Russian roulette with his best friend when he pulled the trigger and sent a bullet through his own brain. Investigators re-ported the accidental suicide occurred after Helms had watched part two of the "Nightmare on Elm Street" series.

"Friday the 13th" and "Nightmare on Elm Street" are only two of many widely accepted horror movies that attract large audiences. The appearance of local video outlets, whose films are as dazzling as their flashing lights, has provided a new marketplace. Many such videos are low-budget flicks that never reach neighborhood theaters. Yet teens can rent and repeatedly watch these films in the comfort of their homes.

HORROR-FILM CHECKLIST

If your child wants to rent a horror video, here are a few famous classics to avoid:

• "Prom Night" depicts a hooded killer haunting a high-school prom. At one point, a decapitated victim's head rolls onto the dance floor.

• "My Bloody Valentine" shows teenagers trapped in an abandoned mine shaft where they're mutilated and killed by a crazed miner.

• "Madman" is a campfire story about a legendary mad killer who wipes out all but one of the kids at a summer camp.

• "Halloween," one of the originals of the current horror craze, was released in 1978 and cost $300,000. So far, it has grossed over $55 million.[4]

While splatter films cannot positively be blamed for increased interest in Satanism, these movies have taken on new dimensions. In the sixties horror films drew on such classic fiction as Frankenstein, Dracula, or Jekyll and Hyde. Today's movies and videos are more graphically sinister, concentrating on inescapable terror and ghastly revenge. The fixation is not on myth-making and storytelling, but on death and destruction. Virtually without exception, the presence of human kindness and noble values is neither recognized nor desired in such films.

REMOVING THE HORROR FROM YOUR HOME

As a parent, it may be difficult for you to understand why any child would watch such satanic outrage. Some children consider horror movies a rite of passage. Like riding a roller coaster, the trick is to see if you can take it. Some psychiatrists say it's a release for teenagers, a kind of primal therapy. Screaming at the escapades of Freddy and Jason is a way of venting the frustrated forces of sex, violence, and hostility.

Director David Cronenberg, known for his horror flicks "Scanners" and "Video Drome," argues that violence has a purpose beyond shock. Cronenberg says, "In a horror film, you invite people to confront some very disturbing things about the human body, disease, and death in the way they might confront them in a dream. It's an attempt to deal with realities that you normally refuse to face. Every time I kill someone in my movie, I'm rehearsing my own death."[5]

Some mental health professionals disagree with Cronenberg's rationalization. Reflecting on horror movie negativism, Los Angeles psychologist Marilyn Ruman declares, "Morbidity is the opposite side of optimism and hopefulness. We have a sense of not having control and celebrate death instead."[6]

The often chaotic plot lines and disjointed camera sequences of many horror films are randomly based. Instead of fostering mental stability, the cinematic techniques leave movie-goers wondering what will happen next. Such unpredictability enforces morbid fears that young minds cannot process.

Tell the teen who wants to watch horror movies that the human

mind can handle only so much stress before it becomes overbur-
dened and desensitized. Scenes of gore galore can become so indel-
ibly imbedded that the film becomes a living nightmare, triggering
neuroses, trauma, and ongoing phobias. Don't hesitate to declare
something is tragically wrong with anyone who watches a movie
for the thrill of watching blood flow.

Parents are often looking for a rule-of-thumb to judge whether
or not a child should see a certain movie. An important question to
ask is, *Will my child be likely to imitate what is seen on the screen?*

It's important to distinguish between gratuitous violence committed by humans and the science fiction genre where evil is
evoked by mythical monsters. In films such as "Aliens," extraterres-
trial life forms are responsible for movie mayhem. No one is going
to imitate this obviously fictional brutality.

Not everyone who watches slice-and-dice flicks cares to imitate
them. Most will dismiss the vivid realism as clever photography
and scintillating special effects. But a Jerry, the caller who cooked
dog casserole for his wife, or a Mark Branch, who apparently murdered to imitate his hero Jason, is one horror film fan too many.
Before Satanism gets a stronger foothold in Hollywood, the public
must demand action and adventure—without murder and mayhem.

The real problem with violence may not be only on the movie
screen but also in the home. Teens who experience domestic violence are susceptible to acting out the human brutality of a "Friday
the 13th." David, the young Slayer fan, told me his earliest childhood memory was of his drunken father holding a gun to his head
when he was four years old. David chillingly recalls his father
threatening to pull the trigger. No wonder he was so enraged and
ready to embrace evil—even kill for the devil.

Another caller to "TALK-BACK," Jim, remembered his Satanist
parents burning demonic symbols into his arms. As a child he was
forced to drink blood in ceremonies. By thirteen he was inducted
into group sex orgies with both men and women.

"Some of the things I saw were hideous," Jim explained. "Children were made to eat human waste. We were drugged so we'd go
along with what was happening."

What brought an end to Jim's nightmare?

"When I was sixteen I overheard the high priest talk about sacrificing me on my eighteenth birthday," Jim said. "So I ran away and haven't seen or heard from my parents since then."

"Did you have any other family members who were victimized?" I asked.

"Yes. My brother was so brutalized he turned to homosexuality," Jim responded. "He was found tied to his bed and stabbed to death. Someone had tried to cut out his heart with a knife!"

Jim began sobbing. "Every time I see the scars on my body it reminds me of the satanic violence. Psychologically I've dealt with my past, but the marks on my body still serve as physical reminders of what was done to me. It makes me so angry I want to hurt others to get even."

Pat called "TALK-BACK" to find help for escaping the satanic cult of her parents.

"At nine years of age my father started reading pornographic books to me," she declared. "He'd show me pictures and then do the same things with me. He also shared me sexually with his friends.

"I'm four months pregnant with my father's child. But it's not the first time," Pat went on. "I've had four other children by him. They were sacrificed in satanic ceremonies!"

"Why did you continue going along with such abuse when you got older?" I asked.

"If I refused, my father would beat me. He knew just how and where to strike my body so nobody would see the scars and bruises."

"What has this brutality done to you?"

"I've blocked out a lot of it," Pat said. "But the more I remember, the more I hate my father and can't live with myself anymore."

David, Jim, and Pat are dramatic examples of how violence affects its victims. Most parents reading this book aren't involved in such savagery, but that doesn't alleviate their responsibility to ask themselves some sober personal questions:

- What are my child's earliest memories?
- Is my child's mind filled with thoughts of warm relationships that teach openness and honesty?
- Do I give my child opportunities to fail without censure?

• Is my child able to share with me his deepest disappointments and hurts?

• Has my method of child discipline ever gotten out of hand to the point of physical abuse?

Any of these questions which stir alarm should be met forthrightly with honest admissions of failure. Professional therapy may be needed immediately. If a parent lives with a spouse who is violent, seeking the assistance of a shelter or instant intervention by the authorities may be necessary. Violence begets violence. Urgently seeking help to quell domestic chaos may prevent a nightmare on your street.

6

Black Metal Mania

"I'm a Satanist. I hate your God. I listen to black metal music—Slayer and King Diamond. They're my gods. King Diamond rules."

That's the way Lars started our conversation. No words minced. Blunt, direct, frightening. He called "TALK-BACK" several months before I toured with Slayer.

"I was flipping through the radio dial and heard you putting down Satanism over the air," he said. "I called to defend my god.

"I want to go to hell. The Christian Bible says it's a place of fire and brimstone. It's not. That's just the idea of Christians to scare people into believing in God."

"Did God lie in the Bible?" I asked Lars.

He didn't answer, so I turned to the next obvious question. "What's it really like in hell?" I demanded.

"Let me recite you something," Lars responded. "'Down in the depths of my fiery home, someone's bell will chime. Now it's time for your fate, and I won't hesitate to pull you down into this pit.' That's 'Jump in the Fire' by Metallica. What do you think of that, Bob?"

"Not much. How did you get involved in this?"

"I've been evil since a child. I always tried to torture things."

"What's the worst you've done for the devil?"

"Sacrifices."

"What kind?"

"Dogs and cats."

"Will you stop there?"

"Probably not. I have to break all ten commandments. If Satan tells me to murder someone, I will."

I'd heard similar comments from other teens, like David, who professed devotion to the devil. To some, such assertions are expressions of bravado. To others, like Lars, it's a way of verbalizing inexpressible anger. Uttering the unthinkable is the ultimate shock tactic for attention.

Whatever the motive, hearing a teenager confess he'd kill for the devil always chills me. It's usually a hollow threat. But for many of those you will read about in this book, it was a violent pledge they fulfilled. God knows who really means it. I can't recognize who is serious about Satan, so I consider every oath of evil as soberly spoken.

Lars' fascination with such bands as Slayer and King Diamond is not unique. The albums of black metal musicians earn millions of dollars annually. Satanism sells, and someone is buying. Most parents have no idea what is happening. They would easily spot *The Satanic Bible* in their child's bedroom, but most adults have never heard of King Diamond. An album called *Them*, the title for a Diamond record release, could refer to anyone. What parent would suspect that *Them* is written about demons?

Carl Rashcke, director of the University of Denver Institute of Humanities, believes, "You might say heavy metal rock is to self-styled Satanism what gospel music is to Christianity. Very few people get converted to Christianity just by listening to gospel music on the radio. But heavy metal is a very powerful reinforcement. It legitimizes the nasty stuff the kids are already into."[1]

In this chapter, we'll consider some offensive black metal bands that affect teens like Lars. We'll begin with Lars' favorites, Slayer and King Diamond. (Though Chapter 1 deals with Slayer, this chapter looks more closely at Slayer's sway over young fans.)

THE SWAY OF SLAYER

How fitting that Slayer should be one of Lars' gods. One rock periodical called the group the "kings of black metal."[2] The Slayer song, "Altar of Sacrifice," declares, "Learn the sacred words of praise, 'Hail Satan.'" Vocalist and bass player Tom Araya says, "Who needs another love song? We like to explore the dark side of things."[3] When writers from the rock journal *Hit Parader* asked if he worshiped the devil, Araya responded obliquely, "I plead the Fifth on that. I have my own beliefs, and if my beliefs fall in that direction, then maybe I am."

This four-piece band from L.A., with a satanic pentagram as its logo, considers itself the best of black and speed metal, a fast violent style of rock that appeals to punkers, thrashers (skateboarders), and those enamored with Satanism. They feature albums entitled *Show No Mercy, Hell Awaits,* and *Reign in Blood.* Their songs include numbers about blasphemy ("Jesus Saves"), demons ("Haunting the Church"), and sex with corpses ("Necrophiliac"). Their themes of the occult and violence encourage self-destruction and selfish rebellion. As Araya argues, "We're more fascinated with death than anything."[4]

Slayer was blamed for inspiring a Lake City teenager in rural Arkansas to attempt killing his parents by beating them with a club, then slicing them with a butcher knife. The assailant said he consulted a Ouija board and heard voices telling him to murder his parents. When police investigated, they found the teen's cassette player cued to the song "Altar of Sacrifice," from the album *Reign in Blood.* The graphic lyrics propose, "High priest awaiting, dagger in hand, spilling the pure virgin blood. Satan's slaughter, ceremonial death, answer his every command." The teen believed that by offering a human sacrifice he would receive a share of the power that Slayer had.[5]

Youth idolize black metal musicians like Slayer. Unfortunately, few performers seem concerned about how they affect audiences. Slayer has been accused of recording songs that have led to teen suicides. Their response?

"We like to shock people. We write lyrics about blood and death . . . I have no idea why kids commit suicide," lead singer Araya told a reporter. "It might be our song that makes them snap when there's a million other things wrong with them."[6]

Exerting ultimate irresponsibility, Slayer's album *South of Heaven* contains a song entitled "Mandatory Suicide!" Its theme is war, not suicide, though that thematic difference hasn't been noted by many teens who consider it an anthem of self-destruction.

A DIAMOND IN THE ROUGH

And what of Lars' other idol, King Diamond?

Before he became a single act, King Diamond fronted the band, Mercyful Fate. A soccer player from Denmark and a self-confessed Satanist, King Diamond (real name Kim Petersen) has reportedly anointed his audiences with human blood and filled a doll with pig's entrails and sacrificed it. His microphone stand is made of human bones shaped like an upside-down cross. Diamond's on-stage face makeup features black bat wings over his eyes and an inverted cross on his forehead.

On the front of the Fate album, *Metal Forces*, Diamond clutches a nun's bosom and bites her neck, while two streams of blood trickle down her chest. "I deny Christ, the deceiver," Diamond says. "I believe in the philosophy of Anton LaVey. Evil is necessary in the world, or how else could you appreciate good?"[7] His concept album, *Them*, tells of a demented grandmother, tormented by murderous demons. She is released from an asylum and returns home to go on a killing spree, bloodily dispatching Diamond's mother and sister, Missey. She is bent on murdering Diamond too. Tormented by his own demons, Diamond kills his grandmother before he is killed.

Though many black metal bands espouse Satanism tongue-in-cheek, the King is no diamond in the rough. "What you see with me is 100 percent real . . . I do understand the dark side of life. Because I profess being a Satanist doesn't mean I go around killing babies. It simply means I understand the powers of the unknown."[8]

Black metal is more than music. It's an all-encompassing image conjured by the songs' lyrics and the artists' antics. And it's programmed to a young audience. Only 9 percent of heavy metal audiences surveyed are twenty-four years of age or older.[9] Black metal music's accolade to evil is profoundly alluring to disaffected youth who attend concerts where thousands of compatriots flash the "evil hand" satanic salute. But use of evil themes in pop music isn't new. The seeds of Satanism in rock music were sown almost two decades ago.

SATANISM'S ROOTS IN ROCK

Contemporary seeds of Satanism were planted when Mick Jagger leered, "Just call me Lucifer." The peripatetic Rolling Stone requested "Sympathy for the Devil." What baby boomer could forget the early Stones posing as witches for the cover of the album, *Their Satanic Majesties Request,* or *Goat's Head Soup,* the seventies Stones' album that pictures a severed goat's head (the symbol of Satan worship) floating in a boiling cauldron?

LED ZEPPELIN

The tie binding Satanism and rock music is much more obvious than the link between Satanism and occult games or horror movies. Jimmy Page, lead guitarist for the now defunct Led Zeppelin, once owned an occult bookstore that catered to an exclusive clientele. Page also revered the infamous British Satanist, Aleister Crowley. Page bought Crowley's former Scottish mansion, known as Boleskine House. The building features an underground passageway where Crowley allegedly conducted sacrificial ceremonies, including human sacrifices.

Page turned the mansion into a Crowley shrine and tried to contact Crowley's spirit via seances. He even commissioned avowed Satanist Charles Pace to decorate the home with motifs depicting various forms of ritualistic magic. Robert Plant, former lead singer for Led Zeppelin, once shared Page's occult fascination but now refuses to visit Boleskine, believing it curses those who come in contact with it.[10]

Page's fascination with the occult has been blamed for the tragedies that plagued Led Zeppelin. In addition to the alcohol-induced death of drummer John Bonham, Robert Plant's young son, Karac, died of an illness. A Zeppelin roadie also died mysteriously. A 1975 auto accident in Greece seriously injured Robert Plant and his wife. Those close to the band say Jimmy Page spent days in a dark room, candles lit, sitting before a table covered with knives. He would hold his guitar "waiting for something to come through."[11]

What came through Zeppelin was one of the most popular rock classics of all time—"Stairway to Heaven." Proponents of so-called satanic backward masking have declared it contains secret encoded messages to "my sweet Satan." Though such conclusions are linguistically and phonetically dubious, the derivation of "Stairway" is no mystery. Robert Plant avidly read the works of British writer, Lewis Spence, and he openly cited Spence's *Magic Arts in Celtic Britain* as one source for the song's lyrics.

"And it's whispered that soon if we all call the tune, then the piper will lead us to reason," declares "Stairway." Critics of the song, worried about occult inferences, say the "piper" could be Satan. They also point with concern to the lyrics, "you know sometimes words have two meanings" as an indication that Page was inspired by Satanist Aleister Crowley's teachings to imbed the song with hidden messages. Such a conclusion might explain the seemingly metaphysical meaning of the line, "The tune will come to you at last when all are one and one is all."

According to one rock critic, "'Stairway to Heaven' . . . seemed to be an invitation to abandon the new traditions and follow the old gods. It expressed a yearning for spiritual transformation."[12]

MISCELLANEOUS BLACK METAL BANDS

The Rolling Stones and Led Zeppelin established a trend that was imitated by other musicians who helped establish the black metal music tradition. Ritchie Blackmore of Deep Purple and his own band, Rainbow, admits attending seances and practicing astral projection. He denies actual involvement with black magic. Blackmore asserts, "I'm an observer of it, and I'm very interested in psychic phenomena. But I'm not offering up slaughtered lambs . . . and I'm certainly not into Aleister Crowley."[13]

Black Sabbath's initial album featured a witch on the front and a black upside-down cross inside the fold-out front cover. The cover for their album "Born Again" featured a red, demonic baby sprouting claws on its fingers and horns on its head. To Black Sabbath, it may be show biz, but to at least one teenager such imagery was seriously sinister. A fifteen-year-old Michigan youth put a shotgun to his brother's head, blew his brains out, and told authorities, "Black Sabbath made me do it."[14]

Former Sabbath lead singer, Ozzy Osbourne, has spanned nearly twenty years with satanic subjects. He puts inverted crosses on his albums (*Diary of a Madman*), dedicates songs to Aleister Crowley ("Mr. Crowley" on *Blizzard of Oz*), and has spoken openly of demons in "The Devil's Daughter" (*No Rest for the Wicked*).

Though marriage and approaching middle age have slowed Ozzy considerably, his seminal dedication to the devil fueled much of today's pop fascination with evil.

Regarding the early days of Black Sabbath, Ozzy says, "We started developing a fascination with the occult. Tony Geezer was reading every book he could come up with on the subject."[15] At one point, Ozzy wanted to build a black cathedral in his backyard, complete with a magic circle inside. Still, he denies affiliation with evil. "People must understand that when I sing about Aleister Crowley, it's done to be theatrical,"[16] Ozzy argues. "I'm not a maniac devil worshiper. I'm just playing a role to have fun with it,"[17] he contends.

The current domain of black metal is haunted by other equally offensive bands. Rock's symbiosis with Satanism in the past was bad, but what teenagers hear today is notably worse. The verity of Venom, a black metal band, is simple: "The death of your God, we demand. We spit at the Virgin you worship, and sit at Lord Satan's left hand." Venom, featuring one member named Abbadon (after the evil demon of the Revelation), sings "In League with Satan," "One Thousand Days in Sodom," and "Live Like an Angel (Die Like a Devil)." Their tune "Possessed" declares, "Satan as my master incarnate, Hail! Praise to my unholy host!"

Other offensive black metal bands are reviewed in Appendix C, "A Parent's Guide to Black Metal Music." But new groups are forming every day, and only the alert parent can warn his child about offensive rock bands.

Whatever the real intentions of black metal bands, the shocking reality is that their teenage fans often interpret satanic songs in the most gruesome way imaginable. Recently three Missouri youths were charged in the beating death of a fourth. They admitted to being deeply involved with black metal. One claimed his favorite song was Megadeth's "Black Friday ("Their bodies convulse in agony and pain. I mangle their faces 'til no features remain").[18]

LYRICAL DOCTRINES OF DEMONS

Teenagers who call "TALK-BACK" constantly quote black metal lyrics to explain their philosophies of life. They claim the songs and the message of the words inspire their actions. Lars, the teen whose gods were Slayer and King Diamond, told me that he was excited by black metal music's evil ideas. To prove his point, he quoted from a Slayer song:

"Night grows cold, twilight's near. On the edge of madness the wounds are sheared. Forms of hanging flesh, shredded carcass, no spared breath. Imprisoned in a shell ready to explode, dead soul, stone-cold, open to the night."

"It excites me," Lars said. "It makes me feel an inner evil. *The Satanic Bible* says . . . ."

I was uncomfortable with his repetitive recitation of evil, so I quickly butted in. "I don't want to hear what *The Satanic Bible* says. The Bible says to love your enemies."

"Well, if you love your enemies, that's a sign of weakness. Anton LaVey, who wrote *The Satanic Bible*, says so."

Lars was angry. He was doing more than quoting Anton LaVey. He was repeating the litany of evil to cope with the lack of love in his life. I didn't know it at the time, but Lars' dad was an alcoholic who had left home when Lars was only two. His mother, an airline stewardess, had allowed Lars to stay by himself when she was on trips since the time he was eleven. Like many teenagers I confront daily on "TALK-BACK," Lars intuitively knew love was important but didn't know where or how to find it.

I determined to challenge Lars at the point of his greatest need in life.

"Lars, I love you. I care about you."

"I don't love you, Bob. I cut your love off. You don't understand. I kill and destroy. I lie and cheat. Satan is my god."

"Lars, if that's true, the next step is spilling the innocent blood of a human. Then, you'll be totally dominated by the devil."

"That's what I want!"

Lars boasted furiously of his devotion to the devil, and part of Lars meant it. I'd heard the same defiant hatred before from other callers, some of whom criminally acted out their anger. Soon, he could destroy two lives—his own and an innocent victim's. I wanted to stop him.

"I'd like to meet you," I said.

"You can't. You live in Denver, and I live in Canada."

"I'm going to be in your city in a couple of weeks. Will you meet me face-to-face?"

"Sure! You can even meet some of my satanic friends."

"So, Lars, you accept my challenge? Put up or shut up!"

"I'll accept any challenge God gives me. I'll destroy it. I'll jump on it and bite it and make it bleed, because your God Jesus is a liar."

THE CONFRONTATION BETWEEN LOVE AND HATE

Two weeks later, I met Lars in a Vancouver hotel lobby. He looked the part he professed on the phone: long, dyed-black hair, black clothing, and a sinister scowl on his face. But there was a soft, kind look in his eyes that betrayed his insistence on evil. On one arm, he had painted the words, "Evil knows no boundaries." The other arm simply said, "Slayer." He was accompanied by his friend Ron, an older boy, who had introduced him to Satanism.

For two hours, we talked. Not about God. About sports, food, the weather, and his main passion—black metal music. Lars had expected a "Scripture-quoting fundamentalist dressed in a white polyester suit and holding a huge, hardbound Bible." What I expected was a vicious, hateful fifteen-year-old, hell-bent on cursing Christ.

Lars said I was a "pretty cool guy." I saw a hurt young man, neglected much of his life by a divorced mother who had been forced to raise him alone. Lars saw in Satanism an opportunity to express his suppressed hostilities through a religion of rebellion. Black metal music was the crux of his creed. As happens with many teenage Satanists, the connection between Satanism and the power chord catechism of black metal music provided his doctrines.

"What do you think of Metallica's album, *And Justice for All?*" Lars asked.

"At least it's not as bad as their past records," I said. "Those guys are finally singing about subjects of social significance, like the title song.

"How do you feel about Wayne Gretsky coming to the United States to play hockey?" I wanted to know.

"Too bad for us Canadians. But we've still got the best hockey teams in the world," he responded proudly.

Small talk. But it broke the ice. Gradually the conversation became more serious.

"I can't believe you took time to meet me here tonight. No one's ever done that for me before."

"I told you, Lars, I care about you."

"Just remember, I'm a Satanist," he reminded me. "You don't really know me or you wouldn't be so nice to me. I do lots of evil things. All the kids in school are scared of me because of the way I look and act."

"Lars, I'm not afraid of you. The first time we talked, I sensed a softness in your voice behind all the terrible things you were saying. And I see that same gentleness in your eyes tonight."

It had become obvious to me that Lars was a self-styled Satanist. He was not part of a coven and had only used hatred as a substitute for love. I sensed that I might be able to reach him.

"I noticed you were carrying a camera when you came in. Can I have my picture taken with you?" Lars asked. "Then all my friends will believe me when I tell them I actually met Bob Larson, the guy on the radio."

Cr-r-rack! I could almost hear it break. Lars' hard, self-protecting emotional facade was splitting, allowing the light of love to shine through. No one asks to have their picture taken with someone they hate.

We smiled for the camera, and Lars put his arm around my shoulder. A unique chemistry was forming. I really liked Lars, and down inside he was starting to like me.

After the flash went off, something important happened. Lars kept smiling. I had showed him I cared, and it meant a lot to him. Unlike David, the Slayer fan in the first chapter, Lars had less stringent defenses against genuine expressions of affection.

"Will I ever get to see you again?" he wondered. "There are a lot of questions I'd like to ask you."

Simple, ordinary conversation. That did it. On a mundane human level, Lars discovered that Satanism wasn't important when compared with honest communication about real feelings. He began to trust me. That confidence signaled the eventual end of his involvement in Satanism.

HOW TO REACH A TEENAGE SATANIST LIKE LARS

Satanism in popular culture involves more than overt solicitations to the enemy of God. Musicians, artists, and entertainers of all sorts, who glorify the instinctual nature of man, side with Satan. Anton LaVey, founder of the Church of Satan, points out that adoration of unfettered human desire and worship of the self are the same as evoking a malignant personification. Consequently, when an artist sings or speaks of hedonism, licentiousness, or any deviant, felonious deed, he honors the devil.

You must warn your child that songs advocating a party-until-you-drop attitude are also satanic. In addition, when rock artists speak lightly of moral evil, condone violence, or make glib statements about complex problems, they further frustrate the idealistic aspirations of youth. For example, when Ozzy Osbourne calls nuclear war the "ultimate sin" (as he does on an album of the same name) he ignores the need for personal morality based on religious imperatives. These themes are just as potentially emotionally damaging to teenagers as overt lyrical invitations to evil.

Finally, irresponsible pop songs reduce personal and global problems to a short lyric line that amplifies youth's despair. Not every youngster who listens to black metal will embrace Satanism. Perhaps 90 percent of teens who end up in devil worship get involved because it's a fad. But even one teenager swearing an oath to the Prince of Darkness because of black metal mania is one too many.

The cassette or CD player in too many teens' rooms is an altar to evil, dispensing the devil's devices to the accompaniment of a catchy beat. Of course, your average fifteen-year-old isn't going to sacrifice a dog because he heard a Venom album. He won't sell his soul to Satan after hearing King Diamond say Satan is "the power of the universe."[19] But many teenagers are not "average." They do not come from loving homes with laudable parental role models. They often are raised in homes that lack emotional support and positive spirituality.

During my first phone conversation with Lars, I asked him a critical question: "Does anybody love you?"

"No!" he responded bitterly. "I hate my parents! And I hate God! Satan is the enemy of God. All that Satan hates, I hate. All that he loves, I love. I don't want love. I hate love!"

"But, Lars, we all want love. Every psychologist acknowledges that. It's the most fundamental of all human desires."

"The only person I want to be loved by is Satan."

Lars is typical of many teens who replace love with hate. On their own, they explore forbidden and exotic realms of the occult. Waiting around the next corner of their fears and frustrations are exploitive black metal musicians who graphically convey bloody themes of despair and death.

Since meeting Lars in Vancouver, he has called me regularly. He renounced Satanism and struggles with the realization that love, no matter how imperfect, is immeasurably better than hate.

Two turning points in Lars' life are important for parents and teen readers of this book to consider. First, our confrontation in Vancouver changed his perspective on love. I cared enough about him to go out of my way.

Parents need to spend time listening to their child's emotional struggles. Your child's escape from evil may not take long once he knows you are concerned about his fears and conflicts.

The second turning point for Lars took place after I returned from the Slayer tour. Even though he had given up Satanism, Lars clung to black metal mania. He continued listening to Slayer, absorbing their lyrics day after day.

"What did you find out, Bob? Do they worship Satan? I've got the cassettes of their albums in my hands right now. I can't believe they would betray us kids just to put on a front. Do they mean what they sing?"

"No, Lars, they don't," I revealed. "It's all a gimmick to make money. They don't take any responsibility for teens getting into Satanism. Frankly, they don't really care about you."

Cr-r-runch!

I could hear the sound of something being crushed under foot. Then, silence. I realized that Lars was smashing his Slayer cassettes to smithereens. His reaction was similar to David's. Other fans would feel the same way if they understood how callously Slayer has contrived their satanic image.

Parents and counselors must tell teenagers that the black metal idols they worship with posters on their walls and cassettes in their Walkmans don't know they exist. And these black metal stars don't care about the personal hurts and concerns of their fans. Teens are a statistic these stars can milk for money. That's all. They may be gods to the teenager, but the teenager is meaningless to them.

With the exception of a few metal musicians like King Diamond, Satanism is a gambit, a ruse that caters to the baser instincts we all have. Rock stars sing about death and despair. But when the concert is over, they count the cash. Help teenagers wake up to the deception of metal music before they buy into something their rock gods don't believe. If they don't, Satan could claim their souls!

Many disillusioned youth seek control over their neglected, helpless circumstances. For some, like Lars, Satanism seems to be an answer. Its ethic of harm and injury to the innocent is an extreme, flagrant transgression of dearly held societal values. The result, says the songs of black metal, is power over standards of morality and justice. The product is sold without regard for consumer liability, and its shelf-life is short in today's world of immediate gratification. But even the most unruly youth knows it's a poor substitute for real goals in an environment of security and love.

7

Satan's Opiate

A "TALK-BACK" caller named Nancy didn't admit at first that she was involved in Satanism. She started the conversation by saying, "I need some help because I've been hooked on cocaine for over two years."

"How do you get the money for the drugs? Steal?"

"Yes."

"Sell yourself?"

"That too."

"Do your parents know you're hooked on cocaine?" I asked.

"The principal at my school told them, but they just shrugged it off," Nancy responded.

"Do you get along with your parents?"

"Not really. They don't have time for me. The only time they ever told me they loved me was when I got in some deep trouble."

"What kind of trouble?"

"The cops. I got busted for carrying a gun."

"Why were you carrying a gun?" I insisted upon knowing.

Nancy didn't respond. Then in barely audible sighs, I could hear the sound of weeping.

"Are you crying?" I asked.

"You asked where I got the money for cocaine. Well, most of the time I get the drugs for free. I know some guys involved in Satanism. When I need some drugs, they come around. They take me places and get me stoned so I'll perform sexually for them."

"What kind of places?"

"Where they hold ceremonies."

Nancy's voice started to tighten. It was a difficult conversation for her. "What kind of ceremonies?" I insisted upon knowing.

"Animal . . . and human," she blurted out.

"When was the last time you saw them kill someone?"

"The first time, it was an infant. Two weeks ago, they sacrificed a six-year-old child. Afterwards, they warned me they'd sacrifice me too if I ever told anyone."

DRUG-DEALING MURDERS IN MATAMOROS

The sobering reality of the connection between drugs and Satanism was dramatically driven home in April of 1989 when fifteen bodies were unearthed in Mexico, across the border from Brownsville, Texas. A Matamoros, Mexico, drug ring had kidnapped and murdered innocent victims as sacrifices to Satan. The drug dealers hoped that in exchange the devil would grant them protection from the police and immunity from any bullets fired their way.

Police described the crime scene as a "human slaughterhouse." They discovered a caldron containing blood and bones from the bodies. The heads of some victims had been cut open and the brains removed, to be mixed in the bloody caldron. Before the bodies were buried, wires were attached to the spines, so that they could be pulled out later and made into necklaces.

The case cracked open when they abducted and sacrificed Mark Kilroy, a twenty-one-year-old student at the University of Texas-Austin. Kilroy was in Matamoros partying during spring break and was last seen drinking with friends. His parents searched for weeks, distributing more than twenty thousand handbills and offering a fifteen-thousand-dollar reward for information.

When the truth of his murder was finally known, Mrs. Kilroy concluded, "I think the suspects must be possessed by the devil. That would be the only explanation for such bizarre actions."[1]

James Kilroy said his son's death should show that even casual drug use can led to deadly consequences. "Marijuana is what killed Mark,"[2] he told the press.

THE CHIEF DEPUTY'S VIEW OF THE
MATAMOROS MURDERS

The day this story broke nationally, I interviewed on my radio program Carlos Tapia, Chief Deputy of Cameron County, Texas, where Brownsville is located:

LARSON: "What startled you the most when you saw the crime scene?"

TAPIA: "I thought in my twenty-two years of law enforcement, I had seen everything. I hadn't. As we drew near, you could smell the stench . . . blood and decomposing organs. In a big, cast iron pot there were pieces of human bodies and a goat's head with horns."

LARSON: "What went through your mind?"

TAPIA: "When we saw the bodies, the suspects were laughing and making jokes. They had a very nonchalant attitude."

LARSON: "Didn't they understand the gravity of what they had done?"

TAPIA: "In their wicked, distorted minds there was no seriousness. They thought they had performed some kind of heroic deed for the devil. They believed that by sacrificing innocent human beings, their loads of marijuana would have an invisible shield of protection from law enforcement officers. They were moving an average of one thousand pounds a week across the border."

LARSON: "You must be incensed at what happened."

TAPIA: "I was angry when I heard what they did to a private investigator working for the father of the American boy they murdered. They cut the skin off the bottoms of both his feet and made him walk on salt. Then they put him in a tub of water and boiled him alive. While he was screaming, they pulled pieces of raw flesh off his body."

LARSON: "Any advice for our audience?"

TAPIA: "Don't get caught unawares like we did. If you see any signs of something that's out of the ordinary, notify your law enforcement officers. Do yourself a favor. Save your kids!"

TEXAS STATE ATTORNEY GENERAL'S
COMMENTS ON THE CRIME

I also talked with Jim Mattox, the Texas State Attorney General in charge of handling the investigation of the Matamoros cult crimes.

"What about the link between drugs and this terrible tragedy?" I asked.

"Drug money provided the leader of this cult with the charisma and trappings of prosperity that attracted young men seeking to get ahead. Then, he used Satanism to put some kind of spell on them. As a Christian, I believe that the devil possessed these murderers."

"Mr. Mattox, you've talked to the suspects. What are they like? What kind of person gets involved in drugs and Satanism?"

"They came from fine families. One was head of a soccer team. Another, the head of an aerobics program. They did all the right things and appeared to be loving, kind, and generous people.

"What I saw in Mexico was unbelievable," Mattox went on. "My concern is for the growing influence of Satanism. In a civilized nation, this should not be tolerated."

THE LINK BETWEEN SATANISM AND DRUGS

Drugs and Satanism have been uniquely joined for centuries. Archaeologists note that pre-Columbian cultures forged a link between sadism, terrorism, and human sacrifice by taking drugs. The Meso-American folk religions of the Mayas and Aztecs required human sacrifices and used drugs to induce apathy in the victims.

The writings of Carlos Castaneda, whose books give glowing tales of pharmacological indulgence through the sorcerer Don Juan, have provided a societal backdrop for drugs and Satanism. Castaneda, author of *Journey to Ixtlan, The Power of Silence,* and *The Fire Within,* idealizes black magic practices of human-animal communication and spell-casting. He points out that all such occult procedures are possible under the influence of hallucinogenic drugs such as psilocybin and peyote. Many teenagers have read his books and imitate Castaneda's fusion of the occult and narcotics.

Before fourteen-year-old Tommy Sullivan, the teen Satanist murderer we will meet in Chapter 8, killed his mother and committed suicide, he made a pact with the devil. "I will tempt teenagers on earth to have sex, have incest, and do drugs,"[3] he wrote.

For many participants in satanic ceremonies, like Nancy, the lure of drugs is an enticement attracting them to Satanism. Once involved in the cult, the use of drugs, along with hypnotic suggestion, becomes a form of brainwashing. Satanic cult leaders know that even though their philosophy is based on moral anarchy, they must maintain cohesiveness with their followers. Drugs render the devil's devotees addictively dependent and less likely to abandon their allegiance to Satan.

Mind-altering substances, combined with the charismatic control of an influential cult leader, trap Satanists, leaving them no way out. Ironically, the cult leader seldom uses drugs. To do so would risk losing control over members who are under the influence of drugs. By staying sober, he can better manipulate the group.

The lure of Satanism is selfishness, the same gratifying impulse that causes many to turn to drugs. Thus, an unholy bond exists between drugs and the devil, narcotics being both a form of seduction and a means of continued entrapment. Some Satanists avoid drugs after commitment to devil worship. To them, swearing allegiance to Satan is a more effective high than psychoactive substances. The result is what one social expert calls a "delusional habit of the mind."[4]

As with the Brownsville case, some clandestine devil worshipers become involved in drug trafficking. New inductees may serve as "mules," carriers who transport the drugs across borders and state lines. The illicit distribution of drugs generates an underground cash economy, enabling cult members to spend their time pursuing satanic activities.

A DETECTIVE'S VIEW OF DRUGS AND THE DEVIL

Detective Lt. Larry Jones, an eighteen-year police veteran and director of the Cult Crime Impact Network, strongly believes that drugs and Satanism are inseparable. During a "TALK-BACK" interview, he described why that link is so important.

"People with an inner pain often turn to drugs. But it doesn't work. It creates a bondage to the supplier," Lt. Jones explained.

Though he didn't know Nancy, he described her situation completely. "If you have a satanic group supplying the drugs for you, it's easier to go to their meetings than steal the dope. Also, a certain amount of deadening of the sensibilities is necessary in order to get new cult members to go through what they have to endure."

During my conversation with Nancy she had talked about the horror of seeing children sacrificed for the devil.

"The only way I could cope with what I saw was to do drugs even more," she explained. "I would get so stoned I wasn't fully aware of what was happening at the time. Somehow I would get home and end up in bed. Later I would remember the awful things I saw."

Detective Jones talked more about the use of drugs as a means of coping in cults. "Drinking blood is distasteful to any normal person, yet that's what is required to join some satanic cults. Drugs make it possible to do the unthinkable. Also, many new members have to cut or torture themselves to prove their devotion to the devil. Drugs help them withstand the pain.

"Once they become an active member of the cult, drugs become even more necessary to heighten the mystique of some ceremonies," Jones declared.

I wanted to know if Detective Jones had any advice for teenagers to help them avoid becoming involved in a satanic cult.

"Be careful of anyone who offers you drugs," he said. "For example, you may be at a party and someone takes you into the back room to get introduced to some heavier drugs. Or you may meet someone who seems like a super friend who always has drugs available. He may be trying to draw you into Satanism."

Detective Jones continued his warning. "The more you do drugs, the less you are able to think clearly. Then you become less aware of what is being done to entice you into Satanism."

DRUGS AND EVIL

Eugene Frank Thompson, age twenty, was a small-time burglar and a big-time cocaine addict. On March 23, 1989, Thompson injected cocaine twenty-thirty times during a four-hour period. Moments later, he armed himself with a semi-automatic machine pistol and went on a murderous rampage. A few hours later he ended his own life after killing two women, raping another, and wounding two police officers. Unquestionably drugs pushed him over the edge of insanity into ultimate evil.

The evil of drugs often strikes the most innocent. According to the National Committee for Prevention of Child Abuse, more than 1,200 children in the United States died last year at the hands of child abusers, many of them drug addicts. Of thirty-two states providing information about problems linked to child abuse, twenty-two cited substance abuse "as the dominant characteristic among their caseload." In the District of Columbia, almost 90 percent of reported child abusers are active substance abusers.[5]

The case of Douglas Alan Dale was particularly pathetic. Police found the eighteen-month-old boy screaming after eating four cubes of crack cocaine. The child's mother testified that the morning after a party in her apartment, young Douglas wandered into a bedroom where her boyfriend was sleeping with cocaine nearby. The child began hallucinating after stuffing the cocaine into his mouth.

One tragedy of evil's onslaught through drugs is the way children are forced to become caretaking adults in drug-abusive families. Recently, California authorities were stunned when thirteen-year-old Deanna Young of Tustin turned in her own parents for illicit drug usage. After hearing an anti-drug lecture at her church, Deanna walked to the local police station and turned over a bag containing $2,800 worth of cocaine. In Los Angeles a musician discovered he had been turned in by his eleven-year-old daughter who reported pot plants growing in the backyard.

SANDRA'S STORY OF SATANISM AND DRUG ABUSE

Seventeen-year-old Sandra's situation of parental drug abuse was even more frightening. She and her mother had contacted us for help to escape oppression inflicted by a frightening satanic cult. What she shared was appalling and almost unbelievable.

After a bitter divorce and custody battle when Sandra was nine years of age, her father took her to another state in an attempt to remain her sole guardian. One night, Sandra's father awakened her and took her naked downstairs to a room filled with dirt. He told Sandra, "Your mother is dead and buried there. Dig and find her."

Sandra frantically tried to unearth her mother. When she was unsuccessful, he declared, "Well, I guess she doesn't want you to find her." Then he raped her.

From that point on, Sandra's father continued to commit incest regularly. One evening he blindfolded her, dressed her in white, and took her to an unknown location. He led her to a basement and removed her blindfold.

"There was a pentagram on the floor and the room was painted red and black," she told me. "People were standing around me wearing robes with hoods. I thought I was at some kind of costume party."

"When did you realize something strange was happening?" I asked.

"They told me to lie on the floor and brought out a lamb, a couple of cats, and some rabbits. A man cut open the animals and let the blood drain down on my white dress. This man had a veil over his face, but when he bent over to drip the blood on me I recognized him as the pastor of a Christian church my father had taken me to!"

"How did you react to what was happening?"

"I was in shock. I cried hysterically. I thought if I laid still and went along with it they might quit. Finally, they were finished and everyone congratulated me. My dad put the blindfold on me and walked me back to the car."

"Did they ever explain to you what it was all about?"

"I suppose it was some kind of ceremony marrying me to Satan."

"Did your father ever share you sexually with others?"

"Yes. Sometimes I was forced to participate sexually in rituals. Even my grandfather and grandmother had sex with me as part of satanic ceremonies. They kept saying this is what happens in close families."

"Nothing much different happened until I was thirteen. Then there was a human sacrifice. He was an adult and they cut him open with a knife and removed his heart. They cut it in pieces and passed it around and ate it."

"Did you eat it?"

"Yes. What else could I do? They forced me. They said that no one would ever believe me if I told them what I saw, and they threatened to kill me if I tried to escape."

"Didn't the victim of the sacrifice try to escape?" I wanted to know.

"He didn't seem willing, but they didn't have to restrain him. He appeared apathetic. I think he was drugged because my dad had me on drugs when he took me to rituals, and that's how I acted."

"Were you drugged that night?"

"Yes. My father injected me with drugs all the time. He used a heavy hypnotic drug combined with valium and heroin. It heightens your senses but relieves anxiety. That's how I was able to cope with what was going on and not go crazy. I don't know how I would have handled the sacrifice if I hadn't been drugged."

"What do you remember most about it?"

"His heart. I used to think that the insides of people looked like heart-shaped pictures . . . like a valentine."

"What happened after the sacrifice?"

"They wiped up the blood. I walked up to the body to feel his flesh. I wanted to make his pain go away, but I couldn't touch him. It was too gross.

"Some of what happened is hard to remember because of the drugs. Even though I tried to resist being injected, I didn't have a choice."

"Did you ever have to witness a human sacrifice again?"

"Yes. Twelve times in all. I'm sorry, I really can't talk about all of them now. It's too painful."

SEAN SELLERS AND DRUGS

While many teenage Satanists are drawn to the devil by drugs, that wasn't the case with Sean Sellers, a Satanist who murdered three people and whose story you'll read in the next chapter.

From his Oklahoma State Penitentiary Death Row cell, he told our "TALK-BACK" audience, "I liked my mind and body and didn't want to abuse it. But after I got into Satanism, I changed. I adopted the attitude, 'If it feels good do it.'

"The first time I ever got high was after a ritual. I rolled marijuana joints with some friends. I had never smoked pot in my life, so it really affected me. I wiped out like I was drunk. The whole room was spinning."

"Did you ever encourage others to use drugs?"

"No. As a Satanist, I wanted everyone to do things voluntarily. Drugs weren't pushed, but they were always around. Eventually, I used to get high during lunch at school and at parties . . . speed and drugs. Drugs didn't bring me to Satanism; Satanism brought me to drugs."

DRUG BABIES

One of my favorite people in the whole world is Mother Clara Hale of Harlem, New York. Mother Hale is an octogenarian black lady who lives in the midst of a New York inner city ghetto that looks like postwar, bombed-out Berlin. Though her surroundings are austere, inside the walls of her Hale House for Children there is more love than I've ever felt anywhere. This remarkable lady, who was honored by former President Ronald Reagan as a national hero, cares for the outcasts of society, tiny babies born to drug-addicted mothers.

When the babies are born, they are also addicted. At a time when most children are teething, these infants are still suffering withdrawal and delirium. Mother Hale invited me to her home to observe her incredible work. Kneeling on the floor, I reached out to hold one of her brood.

She pointed to the doll-sized black baby in my arms. "That infant was just days old when he came here. He slept in a crib in my room every night for the first six weeks. Sometimes he stares off in the distance, and I know he's going through awful pain. His mind has been permanently affected because his mother was a crack addict."

Mother Hale pointed to a tiny Hispanic girl. "See her head drooping to one side? She's nodding off like an adult cocaine addict."

A nurse didn't move quite fast enough and Mother Hale implored, "Quick. Grab her before she falls off the chair."

My eyes welled with tears.

Mother Hale reached out to hug me reassuringly and said, "We have to wake them when they nod off. If we don't, they may fall asleep permanently. One died in my arms a few days ago."

Later that day I visited Harlem Hospital, site of the world's largest pediatric AIDS ward. Dr. Margaret Heagarty, head of the department, showed me rows of cribs containing dying infants, victims of AIDS because their mothers were intravenous drug users. In the critical care section, we saw the worst of them. None was expected to live. They had been left there to die, as peacefully as possible.

One spindly child tried to move about in a walker. His eyes glared wildly. "Dementia has already set in," Dr. Heagarty said.

Many lay under oxygen tents, breathing their last gasps under the constant gaze of loving nurses. I watched one die. The breathing grew slower and slower . . . and then he was gone.

"His mother mainlined cocaine," Dr. Heagarty said. "She couldn't care for him so she left him with us. We used to get them deposited here at six or seven months, but now we're seeing them right after birth."

With the courage of a medic at the front of a battle, Dr. Heagarty looked at me seriously and said, "As a society we will be judged by how we treat the most innocent and helpless among us."

Her words reminded me of what the Brownsville, Texas, police deputy, Carlos Tapia, said as he thought back over the bodies unearthed in Matamoros, Mexico: "Save your kids," he pleaded.

It occurred to me that the killing fields near Brownsville are not really that far from Harlem hospital, and that Satan's opiate, unless it is purged from our midst, may surrender our entire society to Satan.

WHAT TO DO IF YOU SUSPECT DRUG ABUSE

This chapter might alarm some parents who will immediately suspect Satanism if they have detected the possibility their child is on drugs. Such a conclusion may be unwarranted, and making that assumption too quickly could be harmful. There are constructive steps parents can take if they think a child is involved with drugs.

Though the drug problem in America is tragic, the majority of teenagers do not have serious problems with illegal substances. In fact, the most dangerous and widely used drug among teens is alcohol. Advertisements depict beautiful women and athletic men drinking booze and seeming to get the most out of life. The result is a desensitization to abusive substances. Apart from such glamorization, teenagers use drugs for other reasons.

A published survey revealed that 50 percent of teenagers said they used drugs to experiment. Twenty-three percent said peer pressure was the main factor influencing them. Fifteen percent cited escapism. Ten percent blamed rebellion. Four percent said they turned on simply because drugs were readily available.[6]

If you're concerned that someone you love is on drugs, here are the main ones to look for:

• MARIJUANA: Made from the dried leaves of the *Cannabis sativa* plant. Smoked as a cigarette (joint). Tetrahydrocannabinol, the psychoactive ingredient. A gateway drug, introducing teens to other abusive substances. Impairs short-term memory and psychomotor functions. Contains cancer-causing agents. Psychologically addictive.

• COCAINE/CRACK: Highly addictive and potentially lethal. Snorted, smoked, or injected. Stimulant. Affects blood pressure and respiratory system. Crack form highly addictive, causes hallucinations and seizures.

• LSD: Popular hallucinogen during the 1960s, enjoying a resurgence among today's teens. Purchased in dot form, blotted on a piece of paper, and swallowed. Causes panic, paranoia, flashbacks, and sleeplessness.

• PCP (Angel Dust): Hallucinogen that may cause violent behavior. Most often smoked, but also inhaled, injected, or eaten. Causes irrational behavior. Blocks pain receptors, sometimes resulting in self-inflicted injuries. Also known as Loveboat or Graveyard.

• UPPERS: Stimulants such as speed (tablet, pill, or capsule) and crank (white powder and tablets). Sometimes in crystal form, such as crystal meth. Goes by such names as Black Beauties, Footballs, Pep Pills, Bumblebees. Produces anxiety, sleeplessness, and blurred vision. Can cause heart failure.

• DOWNERS: Capsules and tablets producing relaxation but also slurred speech and altered perception in large doses. Depression and comas may result. Both physical and psychological dependence. Goes by such names as Blue Devils, Red Devils, and Yellow Jackets.

• DESIGNER DRUGS: Concocted by underground chemists using unique molecular structure to avoid illegality. May be stronger than the drugs they imitate. Includes synthetic heroin, Ecstasy, China White, and analogs of PCP. Sold as white powder or tablet. Can cause uncontrollable tremors and brain damage.

One problem faced by parents is the teenage myth of "responsible" drug usage. Some youth have the idea that drugs, like alcohol, are all right if consumed infrequently and moderately. The dividing line of danger seems to be the teenage perception of addiction. So long as they are not "addicted," some teenagers feel that drugs are an acceptable form of recreational indulgence. Obviously, such an attitude overlooks serious dangers to health and is based on a highly subjective definition of addiction.

What action should you take on behalf of a teenager using drugs? First check your answers to the following questions:

- Do I drink alcohol to excess and by example convey an image of adult irresponsibility?
- Am I kidding myself by assuming that drugs are a problem in someone else's home and that my child would never get stoned?
- Am I willing to get tough with my child if he's on drugs and do whatever is necessary, including turning him over to the authorities or demanding he undergo special treatment?
- Will I avoid self-righteous lectures and open my heart to the reason my child uses drugs, even if it illuminates my own failure as a parent?

Once you have honestly faced these issues, you are ready to take constructive action to get a teenager off drugs before such abuse leads to Satanism. Deal directly with the problem. The worst mistake is for parents to experience denial and presume the problem is a passing fad. But don't overreact. Calling the police at the first sign of drug paraphernalia or telling your child he has ruined the family's reputation could destroy any later attempt at reconciliation.

Be prepared for your child's vigorous denial. Get some facts from local drug treatment centers to help present your case. Drugs distort moral judgment. Your child's defense may seem preposterous (though it seems logical to him). Be patient. Explain your concerns. Your child may be more addicted than he realizes, and his response could be a distorted interpretation of his physical dependency. You may encounter irrationality and anger. Persist calmly to make your point.

Search your own heart to find your part of the problem. Has love been missing from your home? Is communication an obstacle? Does your child feel neglected? Has an emphasis on social status and materialism bred disrespect for moral convention? Have you blundered by providing inadequate supervision of your child's

spare time? Has your family ignored spiritual values and the importance of regular attendance at church or synagogue?

When the time comes to broach the subject, begin by reaffirm-
ing your love. Assure your child that you want to be part of the
solution. Ask him to point out your failures from his perspective.
Inquire if he comprehends the real reason drugs seem attractive.
Explain that you will not tolerate continued use of illegal and self-
destructive drugs. Confirm your willingness to find the proper
kind of therapeutic treatment to overcome the dependency.

Be ready for one of several arguments:

"The drugs aren't mine, they belong to someone else."

"I'm not hooked because I only use them occasionally."

"It's no different from the booze you drink or the pills you take."

"I only go along with it to be popular."

Drug abuse is a symptom, not a cause. Idle time is the devil's
playground. Organize family activities to keep your child busy. Get
him involved in community efforts to help the needy. Talk with
your church or synagogue about youth activities that combine
spiritual and recreational interests. If necessary, insist that your
child break off relationships with friends who use drugs. Take him
to concerts with you instead of dropping him off to see a heavy
metal band where drug use will be rampant. Talk with his teachers
about special efforts to improve his poor schoolwork.

If your child is uncooperative, professional intervention or an
austere rehabilitation program may be necessary. The situation
may be too far advanced for parental intercession and require
medical treatment and controlled supervision.

Remember, drugs can be an introduction to the occult, the door-
way to the devil and death. Firm discipline, loving acceptance, and
constant vigilance can prevent your child from getting hooked on
Satan's opiate.

PART THREE

Dancing with the Devil

8

Servants of Satan

"I renounce God! I renounce Christ! I will serve only Satan. Hail Satan! Those are the words I wrote in my own blood . . . That night I did a ritual based on the pact and called up the spirits, asking them to enter my body when I went to sleep. I started having a dream about killing my parents. But when I woke up, it was no longer a dream. It really happened."

I had heard similar stories from callers on my talk show and wondered if the tales were true. This time, the "TALK-BACK" caller was Sean Sellers, who was convicted in 1986 at age sixteen of three murders. He is the youngest inmate on Death Row in the Oklahoma State Penitentiary.

A listener of "TALK-BACK with Bob Larson" contacted the state penitentiary chaplain to arrange for Sean to be on the show. Then the chaplain called to see if we wanted to interview Sean.

I was most interested in talking with Sean because I had read about his trio of murders. He killed his first victim, a convenience store clerk, on September 8, 1985. The clerk, Robert Bowers, had once refused to sell beer to Sellers and a companion, Richard Howard. Howard stole his grandfather's .357 Magnum, and the two hunted Bowers down. Sean shot once and missed. He shot again and missed. Bowers tried to escape, but Howard blocked his way. The third shot hit and splattered blood against the wall and floor. Sean and Richard walked out, taking no money or merchandise— only the life of an innocent man.

On March 5, 1986, Sean shot his parents. Sean described the events of that night when he called "TALK-BACK."

"I was very angry with them [my parents] about some problems related to a girlfriend," Sean said. "I went through my nightly satanic devotions by undressing and putting on black underwear and a black, hooded cape. I lit candles and incense. Then I invoked my main spirit, Ezurate, and fell asleep.

"I don't remember anything else until I walked into their bedroom. I had my stepfather's .44 revolver. I'm still not clear how I got it. I shot them both in the head."

He continued. "Then I left the bedroom. A little later I came back and turned the light on. I stood in front of my mother and watched the blood pour out of her onto the bed. Then I laughed and giggled. I felt like a big rock had been lifted from my shoulders—like a burden was finally freed from me."

Sean's story may be dramatic because of his age, but Sellers' methodical involvement in Satanism and his brutal homicidal acts are not unusual in the annals of criminal Satanism. The likes of Charles Manson, Ricky Kasso, and Richard Ramirez, the killers mentioned in Chapter 2, are the tip of the devil's iceberg in hell.

Teenage Sacrifices for Satan

Theron Reed ("Pete") Roland II was a tall, dark, handsome boy everyone considered a basic all-around good boy. On December 6, 1987, Pete and three other boys, James Hardy, Ron Clements, and Steven Newberry, drove to a wooded area near Carl Junction, Missouri. They sacrificed a cat to honor the devil. Suddenly, three of them turned on Steven Newberry.

"Sacrifice for Satan," they chanted.

Frightened, Newberry started running. The three picked up baseball bats, which were part of the ritual, and began striking their comrade. One bat broke. Seventy blows later, Newberry was dead. Pete and his friends dragged the body to a cistern—"the well of hell," they called it. Along with the dead cat they had sacrificed earlier, the young satanic slayers tossed Newberry's body in the cistern.

One baseball bat belonging to Ron Clements had written on it "the ultraviolence stick," a phrase borrowed from the movie, "A Clockwork Orange," about violent gangs in England. When it was over, Pete said he had expected the devil to appear and grant all of them great powers. Instead, Pete and his two friends got life in prison without possibility of parole.

In court, the jury was shown a box with Pete Roland's prized possessions—a satanic notebook with demonic doodlings, a carved skull with a nail driven through it, and diabolical-looking rock posters and album covers. Clements' attorney claimed his client's favorite metal band was Megadeth. His favorite song was their tune, "Black Friday," suggesting, "My hammer's a cold piece of blood lethal steel. I grin while you writhe in the pain that I deal."[1] Reporting on the incident in *Woman's Day* magazine, writer Claire Safran ended her analysis with the poignant question, "If no one is looking, does evil become contagious?"[2]

TOMMY SULLIVAN'S SLIDE INTO SATANISM

Perhaps the most celebrated story of teenage Satanism is the much-publicized account of fourteen-year-old Tommy Sullivan. Raised a devout Roman Catholic, Tommy was described by friends as a poetic person with deep feelings. His favorite rock group was Suicidal Tendencies. His bedroom wall sported posters of Ozzy Osbourne. In a special notebook, his very own *Book of Shadows*, he had written, "To the greatest of demons. I would like to make a solemn exchange with you. If you will give me the most extreme of all magical powers, I will kill many Christian followers. Exactly twenty years from this day, I will promise to commit suicide. I will tempt teenagers on earth to have sex, have incest, do drugs, and worship you. I believe that evil will once again rise and conquer the love of God."[3]

Friends say Tommy's descent into evil began when a teacher requested students to prepare a report on Satanism. For Tommy, the assignment became an odyssey into the occult. The fourte-year-old spent days listening to a growing collection of heavy metal records and became absorbed in playing Dungeons & Dragons. Tommy learned to write backwards and inscribed in his *Book of Shadows* the words, "Evil of all mankind dwells within my soul. If you want in, let me know."[4]

His artistic side was visible in the sinister drawings in the *Book of Shadows,* which contained devilish creatures and scenes of sadistic rituals. One page was entitled "Come to Satan." On another page, a demonic figure held an upside-down cross, standing in front of a woman lying prostrate on a slab being lowered by pulleys into hell.

Finally, Tommy told his friends about a dream in which Satan appeared to him. "Satan had my face," the eighth-grader declared. "He was carrying a knife, and he told me to 'preach Satanism to other kids, and then kill everyone in your family.' "I'm going to do this."[5]

One night shortly after that, Tommy headed for the downstairs den to watch the horror movie "Friday the 13th" on the VCR. At 10:30, his father heard a smoke alarm go off and called the police. When authorities arrived, they found the house splattered with blood. Tommy's mother was discovered with her throat slit and dozens of slashes made with the thrust of a knife. Tommy had tried to gouge out her eyes, and her hands were partially severed.

The next day, authorities found Tommy buried in a snowdrift. His wrists were cut and his throat had been slashed from ear-to-ear with an intensity that nearly decapitated him. Beside him lay the open Boy Scout knife that he had used to kill his mother and end his own life.

DERECK SHAW'S SATANISM

In another tragic case of teenage Satanism, a Sackville, Nova Scotia, sixteen-year-old named Dereck Shaw phoned his girlfriend while her parents were out and told her that on the previous night he had been visited by Satan. According to Shaw, the devil appeared in a blue light and demanded his soul. After speaking with his girlfriend, Shaw told his half-brother and step-brother, both eight years old, to close their eyes while he went to his parents' bedroom and got his stepfather's hunting rifle. He carried the gun down to his bedroom in the basement and put the .30–.30 rifle barrel into his mouth and fired.

Dereck's parents bravely stepped forward to alert the press. They blamed their son's death on his two-year fascination with satanic worship and ritual violence. Just months before, they had confiscated Dereck's black candles, a handdrawn pentagram, and instruction books by which he had apparently conducted rituals. The pastor of Dereck's parents, Reverend Hedley Hopkins, succinctly stated, "Young people who are bored are trying to make contact with evil. And if you try long enough, you eventually find something intelligent and malignant and destructive."[6]

Who are the youth most susceptible to Satanism?

The devil's disciples are mostly middle-class and white. A high percentage are male because of the macho posturing required for blood-spilling rituals and acts of desecration. They are also often creative and intelligent. They are almost always victims of familial alcohol abuse, physical violence, and neglect. Some are leaders of cults, but most are influenced by older, big-brother figures who have already blazed a trail of devilish dissipation.

Satanism supplies young people with an anything-goes invitation. The occult world of mystery and magic becomes real. When confronted about their menacing behavior, they often claim their pursuit of evil is no more perilous than corruption in high places and man-made disasters like Bhopal and Chernobyl.

SOWING THE SEEDS OF SATANISM

Authorities agree that 95 percent of kids involved in the sinister subjects we discussed in part two—drugs, black metal music, fantasy role playing games, horror movies, and devilish paraphernalia—never step beyond the bounds of occult curiosity. Perhaps 5 percent dabble in serious Satanism. But the 1 or 2 percent who go on into the dark realms of soul-pacts and demonic conjurations are grabbing headlines:

- "SATANIST, 15, TOP SUSPECT IN VANDALISM"
- "TROUBLED TEENS TURN TO CULTS FOR RELIEF"
- "YOUTH OBSESSED WITH SATANISM STABS MOTHER TO DEATH, KILLS SELF"

SEAN SELLERS' SAGA OF SATANISM

Why did Sean Sellers worship the devil? How did he become involved in Satanism?

I asked him those questions when he was interviewed on "TALK-

BACK." He told the story of his childhood and gradual induction into the occult. Sean's parents divorced when he was a toddler. His mother, Vonda, married Paul Bellafatto in 1976. Vonda and Paul often neglected young Sean. They left him with family members as their transient lifestyle took them around the country.

Sean was an exceedingly bright student who read science fiction and supernatural tales. When he was ten, his baby-sitter checked out some satanic books for him at the library. In March 1984, when Sean was fourteen, he was uprooted again when Vonda and Paul deposited Sean with Vonda's sister in Okmulgee, Oklahoma.

"Like all teenagers, I was looking for acceptance," Sean explained. "At thirteen, I had a bad experience with a girl. I was mad at God and shortly thereafter was introduced to a witch who took me in as her apprentice. I ended up praying to Satan and felt a sensation like fingertips touching me everywhere.

"Then," Sean said, "I became obsessively involved with Dungeons & Dragons. I went frequently to the 'Rocky Horror Picture Show' (a rock movie musical based on transvestism, sadomasochism, and other perversions). I met a lot of Satanists there. I identified myself by wearing my left shirtsleeve rolled up and keeping my left pinkie fingernail unclipped and painted black. Through Ninjitsu, I delved into the violent aspects of the martial arts, learning how to conceal weapons and commit assassination. I once ate the leg off a live frog in biology class.

"Drugs played a role, too," Sean went on. "I started out with marijuana. I had such a rigorous routine doing rituals at night that I took speed to keep me going."

THE SLIPPERY STREET TO SATANISM

The Paradise Lost of today's teens is populated by a growing number of fallen angels like Sean Sellers, Pete Rolland, and Tommy Sullivan, who pushed the barriers of youthful insurgence into malevolence and the diabolical. It often begins as morbid curiosity but quickly evolves into a search for the supernatural. Eventually, teenage Satanism becomes the ultimate rebellion. Participants revel in destruction, sensual gratification, and heinous rituals designed to shock adult sensibilities. As one teen put it, "It's a short cut to power, and the only thing you have to do is stick your neck out. It's like the occult version of the Marines: 'Are you man enough for this?' "[7]

The journey often begins with an obsession for black metal music, the kinds of bands talked about earlier. Posters adorn walls, and tapes are usually listened to with headphones to avoid adult objections to the villainous lyrics. Outward trappings may be adopted—black clothing, dyed-black hair, jewelry that includes inverted pentagrams and upside-down crosses, as well as goats' heads and the numbers 666. Tee shirts with images of demons and black metal bands become routine costumes (especially on the third Thursday of each month, a day Satanists dedicate to the devil). Some teens paint their fingernails black, all the better for sporting satanic salutes.

Kids who convince parents their bedrooms are off-limits construct actual altars to the devil. Accoutrements may include chalices, black candles, skulls, knives, bones, and occult books. Some even rob graveyards to obtain actual artifacts. At this stage, drugs often enter the picture, especially amphetamines and hallucinogens. Rituals in which blood is consumed are the next step.

The more serious stage of Satanism starts when kids in the occult begin keeping their own *Book of Shadows,* usually a spiral notebook scribbled with metal rock lyrics, quotes from *The Satanic Bible,* backwards language slogans, satanic symbols, grotesque drawings, and suicide notes or elaborate pacts with demons. (Some of these symbols can be seen on page 109.)

BLOOD RITUALS

One day when we were discussing Satanism on "TALK-BACK," a teen named Israel called the show. He identified himself as a member of a gang called S.O.S., which he said stood for "Servants of Satan."

I wanted to know what he did for the devil to justify a gang name like that.

"I do lots of stuff," Israel responded, "like worship Satan's idols. I listen to bands like Slayer and worship demons."

"What else do you do?"

"We kill dogs, cats—you know, we sacrifice them," he calmly revealed. "We get them from the neighbors. The main thing is to kill them slowly."

"Slowly?"

"Yeah. We put the knife into them in different places and twist it. Then, finally, we put it into the heart."

"Don't the animals cry for help?"

"We tie their mouths shut."

Israel's callousness was riveting.

"Sounds bloody," was all I could say.

"Sure, there's blood all over my hands. It's cool. I like blood on my hands. Afterwards, I go home and go to sleep and forget all about it."

"Who gives you the right to kill innocent animals?"

"Satan," he said. "I've made lots of pledges to him. I've sold my soul to Satan."

Israel's fascination with blood could have been the beginning of even more debased rituals of evil. Bloodlust like Israel's is common among satanic groups. Many ceremonies are centered around the shedding and consumption of blood, both animal and human. Animal sacrifices usually require involvement of each member of the group in killing the creature and tasting its blood. A knife may be handed to all participants and each plunges the blade into the body. Then the blood may be collected in a chalice and shared ritualistically in mockery of Christian communion.

As an alternative, each participant may be required to place his hands in the dead animal's entrails and lick the blood from his fingers. When human blood is ingested, a body part is usually cut or severed. Typically, in more serious ceremonies, a finger is cut off, the blood drained into a goblet, and the flesh eaten. Blood is often mixed with urine.

I asked Sean Sellers if he, too, participated in the bloodlust aspects of Satanism.

"Yes. I started carrying little vials of blood with me all the time, he answered. "I kept some in the refrigerator. I was working in a clinic on weekends and would steal needles for extracting blood and vials to carry it in."

"Did blood give you some kind of high? Where did you get the idea?"

SATANIC SYMBOLS

HORNED HAND

The HORNED HAND is a sign of recognition between those in the occult. It is also used by those at heavy metal concerts to affirm their allegiance to the music's message of negativism.

ANARCHY

The symbol of ANARCHY represents abolition of all law. First used in "punk" music, it's now widely used by heavy metal music fans.

ANKH

The ANKH is an ancient Egyptian symbol for life and fertility. The top portion represents the female, the lower portion the male. This symbol supposedly has magical sexual significance.

CROSS OF CONFUSION

The CROSS OF CONFUSION is an old Roman symbol that questions the validity of Christianity. It is used on albums by the rock group Blue Oyster Cult.

CROSS OF NERO

This symbol represented peace in the early 60s. Among today's heavy metal and occult groups, it signifies the CROSS OF NERO. It shows an inverted cross with a cross anchor broken downward, signifying defeat of Christianity.

PENTAGRAM

The PENTAGRAM (without the circle, the PENTACLE) is used in both Black and White Magic. The top point represents the spirit. The other points represent wind, fire, earth, and water. It is believed to have power to conjure good spirits and ward off evil.

ANTI-JUSTICE

The Roman symbol of justice was an upright double-bladed ax. The representation of ANTI-JUSTICE inverts the double-bladed ax.

BAPHOMET

The upside-down pentagram, often called the BAPHOMET is satanic and represents the goat's head.

SWASTIKA

The SWASTIKA or BROKEN CROSS originally represented the four winds, four seasons, and four compass points. Its arms were at 90° angles turned the opposite way, as depicted here, and turned clockwise, showing harmony with nature. The SWASTIKA shows the elements or forces turning against nature and out of harmony.

"It was called for in some rituals we did," Sean divulged. "It gave me an eery sensation. Like in the horror movies where people say that wickedness is 'delicious.'

"But that's not all. Part of the idea of drinking blood came from the attitude among Satanists that the more bizarre something is, the more evil it is. Drinking blood was something that was disgusting, abhorrent, and condemned by God. So it fit in perfectly with the things I was doing. At first, it was like a thrill. As I got more into it, I began to crave blood."

THE SATANIC BIBLE

Many of the teens who call my radio show mention *The Satanic Bible* as their source of information. Sean Sellers was one of them.

"Halfway through my sophomore year, I learned about *The Satanic Bible*," Sean said. "It seemed like it was all true."

The Satanic Bible, written by Church of Satan founder, Anton Szandor LaVey, is a 272-page diatribe for the devil. Published in 1969, it became an instant best seller, topping the half-million mark. On some college campuses, it outsold the Christian Bible.

The book opens with LaVey's explanation of why he came to accept a hedonist philosophy. As a sixteen-year-old organ player in a carnival, LaVey says he observed "men lusting after half-naked girls dancing at the carnival (on Saturday night), and on Sunday morning when I was playing the organ for tent-show evangelists at the other end of the carnival lot, I would see these same men sitting in the pews with their wives and children, asking God to forgive them and purge them of carnal desires. And the next Saturday night, they'd be back at the carnival or some other place of indulgence. I knew then that the Christian church thrives on hypocrisy, and that man's carnal nature will out!"[8]

Early in the book, the Nine Satanic Statements clarify LaVey's doctrines. I include them below so you can clearly understand the heinous basis for modern Satanism. Being aware will help you recognize such ideas when revealed by someone involved in Satanism. Sean Sellers told my audience, "I would go around quoting 'The Nine Satanic Statements.' I was really studying hard the magical formulas."

Obviously, much of the hatred and violence that become a part of teenage Satanism comes from this book.

The Nine Satanic Statements are:

1. Satan represents indulgence, instead of abstinence.
2. Satan represents vital existence, instead of spiritual pipe dreams.
3. Satan represents undefiled wisdom, instead of hypocritical self-deceit.
4. Satan represents kindness to those who deserve it, instead of love wasted on ingrates.
5. Satan represents vengeance, instead of turning the other cheek.
6. Satan represents responsibility to the responsible, instead of concern for psychic vampires.
7. Satan represents man as just another animal, sometimes better, more often worse than those that walk on all fours, who, because of his "divine spiritual and intellectual development," has become the most vicious animal of all.
8. Satan represents all of the so-called sins, as they all lead to physical, mental, or emotional gratification.
9. Satan has been the best friend the church has ever had, as he has kept it in business all these years.

Those who are familiar with the Bible will note that some of these statements are so diametrically opposed to Christian principles that they often twist biblical statements. Christ told his disciples to "turn the other cheek."[9] *The Satanic Bible* says, "Satan represents vengeance, instead of turning the other cheek."

LaVey goes on to say, "Self-preservation is the highest law. He who turns the other cheek is a cowardly dog."[10]

In Proverbs and in Romans, readers are told: "Therefore if your enemy is hungry, give him bread to eat; and if he is thirsty, give him water to drink."[11] *The Satanic Bible* says, "Satan represents kindness to those who deserve it, instead of love wasted on ingrates."

"Why should I not hate my enemies?" LaVey asks. "If I love them, does that not place me at their mercy?"[12]

Imagine a teen you know repeating these Nine Satanic Statements over and over again in his head as Sean Sellers did.

But *The Satanic Bible* goes much further. Since blasphemy is an integral part of worshiping Satan, LaVey includes outrageous invectives hurled against God. "I dip my forefinger in the watery blood of your impotent mad redeemer, and write over his thorn-torn brow: The TRUE prince of evil—the king of all slaves."

If that isn't offensive enough, he adds, "I gaze into the glassy eye of your fearsome Jehovah, and pluck him by the beard; I uplift a broad-axe, and split open his worm-eaten skull."[13]

Lying and indulgence and the seven deadly sins are condoned throughout *The Satanic Bible,* not just in the Nine Satanic Statements. LaVey's ideology is based on immediate gratification. "Life is the great indulgence—death the great abstinence," LaVey proclaims. "There is no heaven of glory bright, and no hell where sinners roast . . . no redeemer liveth!"[14]

Throughout *The Satanic Bible,* LaVey rails against God like a spoiled child resisting parental instruction. In addition to mocking every cardinal Christian doctrine, LaVey also ridicules white witches for not using their malevolent powers. He provides the "infernal names" of demons and proclaims that Satanists condone any kind of sexual activity, so long as it "involves no one who does not wish to be involved."[15] Even the pain of sadism is endorsed.

Human sacrifice is condoned with a carefully worded qualification. LaVey insists he speaks of "symbolically" destroying the victim "through the working of a hex or curse, which in turn leads to the physical, mental, or emotional destruction of the sacrifice in ways and means not attributable to the magician."[16] "Under no circumstance," LaVey insists, "would a Satanist sacrifice any animal or baby."[17]

In spite of such disclaimers, LaVey carefully describes the "ideal sacrifice" and says these "rabid humans deserve any clobberings they get." Further inflaming his readers, LaVey adds, "Mad dogs are destroyed, and they need help far more than the human who conveniently froths at the mouth when irrational behavior is in order . . . therefore, you have every right to (symbolically) destroy them, and if your curse provokes their actual annihilation, rejoice that you have been instrumental in ridding the world of a pest!"[18] After reading such words, teenagers already steeped in resentment and rebellion could easily assume the right to harm, even murder someone.

The Satanic Bible concludes with detailed instructions on how to conduct a devil-worshiping ceremony. All sources of light, except candles, are prohibited. A nude woman usually lies prostrate, feet pointed north, serving as an altar. The air is purified by the ringing of a bell, and invocations to Lucifer are recited. *The Satanic Bible* includes all ritualistic utterances and paraphernalia, leaving no reader to wonder how he might pursue LaVey's infernal craft. La-Vey also includes the "Articles of Faith" of Satanism, the so-called nineteen Enochian Keys, representing the "satanic paeans of faith."[19] LaVey gives both the invocation to these Enochian Keys in the original Enochian language of evil as well as his own interpretation.

THE SATANIC RITUALS

In 1972, as a companion book to *The Satanic Bible*, Anton LaVey published *The Satanic Rituals*, a how-to guide for Satanists. Claiming that we are living in the Age of Satan, he promises followers the ability to "call the names of the Gods of the Abyss with freedom from guilt and immunity from harm."[20] By following the rites and ceremonies outlined, he offers the reader power and control over his destiny.

LaVey explains that "the productions contained [within *The Satanic Rituals*] . . . fall into two . . . categories: rituals, which are directed towards a specific end that the performer desires; and ceremonies, which are pageants paying homage to or commemorating an event, aspect of life, admired personage, or declaration of faith. Generally, a ritual is used to attain, while a ceremony serves to sustain."[21]

Embracing the ideologies set forth in *The Satanic Bible*, LaVey's *Satanic Rituals* compares ceremonies to a stage play. The ceremonial chamber, a dismal setting accented with demonic symbols, becomes the stage. Candles provide an additional mystic ambiance. The priest and his helpers are the main characters, and the play's participants are the audience. They are often attired in dark, hooded robes. Success hinges upon the strength of the participant's belief and magical abilities. LaVey contends, "One of the most important 'commandments' of Satanism is: Satanism demands study—not worship!"[22]

In addition to blasphemy, there is blatant pornography and sexism throughout *The Satanic Rituals*. Often, the altar is a naked woman. Sexual acts are common: "The (L'air Epais) ceremony of rebirth takes place in a large coffin. The coffin contains an unclad woman . . . whose task is to awaken lust in the 'dead' man who joins her . . . When the infusion is complete, the woman within shouts . . . 'Enough!'"[23] Perverted behavior is condoned: "An exclusively homosexual group can often conduct more fruitful rituals than a group with both heterosexual and homosexual participants. The reason is that each person in an all-homophile group is usually more aware of the individual active/passive propensities of his associates."[24] LaVey calls upon ancient, paganistic rites, such as the Seventh Satanic Statement in which participants "regress willingly to an animal level, assuming animal attributes."[25] LaVey also gives explicit instructions for conducting the Black Mass, made famous in the seventeenth century by drug peddler and abortionist Catherine Deshayes.

The Satanic Rituals concludes with a final commentary LaVey calls "The Unknown Known" in which he prophesies, "The twentieth century has prepared us for the future and the coming of the Age of Fire . . . The infant is learning to walk, and by the first Working Year of his age—that is to say 1984—he will have steadied his steps, and by the next—2002—he will have attained maturity."[26]

LaVey's philosophy quite naturally leads to crime and violence. Satanists are determined to break all of the Bible's Ten Commandments and violate the seven deadly sins: pride, lying, murder, a wicked heart, quickness to do evil, a false witness, and causing discord.[27] Consequently, ritual sacrifice (in which blood is consumed), uninhibited violence, and the celebration of selfishness are assiduously followed. Generally, such perpetrators aren't part of any organized satanic clique, but follow a self-styled route to evil.

PARENTAL PROTESTS AGAINST THE DEVIL

If you as a parent sense that any of these indicators are present in your home, act quickly. Anywhere along this pathway, a teenager exploring Satanism is but a moment away from tipping over the edge into demonic delusion. Never pass off such youthful diversions as harmless inquisitiveness. For some, of course, it's only a joke, a way to outrage adults. To them, the devil is only a metaphor for excessive behavior. But to that one teen in a hundred, who could be your child, Satan may be an earnest religious reality and the source of ultimate evil. When they call Satan, it may be a plea for attention. But the devil may answer if you don't first heed their cry for help.

Don't underestimate the powerful influences of black metal music. If you permit metal music in your child's library, you may discover such lyrics are the source as well as the indicator of serious psychological problems. Imagine what would happen to your psyche if you heard Venom sing again and again, "Satan, Father, help me from this grave. Demons, warriors, ever be my slaves. I can raise the fist of hell and blasphemy. We can grow strong, satanic royalty." ("Die Hard")

Parents must comprehend the enticements that draw teenagers to Satanism. The most important lure is power. Our society offers youths unprecedented freedoms, but little real power commensurate with their emancipated state. Cults of the devil promise power over parents, school, and enemy peers. Satanism also pledges permissiveness. Teenagers can act on their hormonal impulses without guilt or acknowledgment of parental values. Finally, evil has a scary, spine-chilling appeal. The risk of evoking evil is an adventurous high. It becomes addictive because of the adrenalin flow.

I asked Detective Bill Wickersham of the Denver, Colorado, police department and Sandi Gallant, a San Francisco police officer who specializes in satanic crimes, "Why do teenagers seem so susceptible to Satanism?"

"I will never forget what one teenage Satanist told me," the detective responded. "He said, 'What is there to live for? We're going to live for today and do what we want. There's no future!'"

Detective Wickersham continued. "In a way, they're right. Look at our society. The divorce rate, kids living with single parents, or both parents working to make a living. There's no family life. Kids have too much idle time. The kids have a point. What the hell is this world coming to?"

Sandi Gallant's answer was much the same. "Our world is an apathetic place," Gallant said. "We are more concerned with ourselves than each other. We live in a violent, negative society. Kids see that as a normal way of life and consequently are drawn into Satanism."

"How does a parent spot the child on the road to Satanism?" I asked her.

"They are often fearful and anxious about what's going on in the world and can't comprehend it," she answered. "Then they lose themselves in metal music and fantasy, role-playing games. Fantasy and reality become intertwined. Too often, parents don't take this stage seriously enough. They think their children will get over it. Then the parents go into denial and fail to communicate. When that happens, parents will no longer be able to distinguish between normal teenage rebellion and the more sinister aspects of Satanism."

Anton LaVey has his own answer to teenagers' rejection of orthodox religions for Satanism. He argues, "Who in the hell is going to want to be dragged to Sunday school if there's a religion that lets them go to a rock concert, give the sign of the (devil's) horn and have fun doing it? That's a pretty hard act to follow."[28]

Unfortunately, teens who commit crimes for Satan are more than just heavy metal fans. They're avid believers. I asked Detective Wickersham, "Have you talked directly with any of these offenders?"

"Sure," he answered. "It's the same as talking to you. They believe strongly, too. Except their god is Satan."

Danger Signs

How can you spot if your child is that 1 percent in dire danger? Watch for this common pattern of the slide into Satanism:

- Grades drop drastically.
- Isolation, aggression, and anger surface.
- A wider circle of friends is exchanged for a select group belonging to the developing coven.
- Sports and extra-curricular activities are avoided.
- Suicidal thoughts are often expressed or written down in distorted poetic forms.

- Secret agendas are established, often involving unexplained activities during late night hours.
- Self-mutilation is practiced and a calendar of regular rituals is scheduled, such as the one noted in Appendix D.
- Available time is spent devoted to satanic literature, often borrowed from a local library. Books like the *Necronomicon,* written by science fiction writer H. P. Lovecraft (see Chapter 10) and *The Satanic Bible* are devoured.

These danger signs may occur because a teenager has too much time on his hands. An idle mind is the devil's playground. An unchallenged child, unprovoked by constructive activity, is open to the exploitation of evil.

A psychiatrist evaluating Pete Roland, Steven Newberry's satanic murderer, aptly described the young killer's vulnerability to evil suggestions. According to Dr. William S. Logan of the Menninger Foundation, Roland was a "blank slate, waiting for someone to write on it."[29]

Before you dismiss any evil influence as innocuous, remember that the concept of evil triumphing over good and the system of Satan worship aren't ingrained in our culture. Those who worship Satan get the idea through movies, books, music, videos, adult propaganda, or other avenues. Expose the entry and post a STOP sign before your child becomes a servant of Satan.

9

Sacrifice of Innocents

"Your name is what?" I asked incredulously.

"I told you. Number One. That's what I call myself because I'm Number One in my life. Anyway," he said. "I called your talk show to discuss your topic—crimes for the devil."

"Have you killed or would you kill for Satan?" I wanted to know.

"I'd kill instantly. It doesn't have to be for any reason. Not even the devil. Remember, I'm Number One."

"But have you ever killed anyone?"

"I plead the Fifth. Let me ask you. Did you ever kill something yourself? Did you ever feel power when you did it?"

"Only hunting game. Shooting a bird," I answered. "That's not evil. Are you evil?" I challenged.

"What do you call evil?"

"Like harming the innocent," I said. "For example, dealing drugs."

"If that's your idea of evil, I fit," Number One replied.

"How about stealing?"

"In a heartbeat. If I wanted something in your car, I would bust open your window and take it."

"Do you have any morals?"

"My only moral is that I'm Number One. If what I do is wrong, why do I feel so great when I kill? Why do I smile?"

I wasn't quite prepared for his follow-up question. "Have you ever tasted blood? Have you ever run your hands through warm guts?" Number One asked.

The on-the-air conversation was getting out of hand. I turned

118

Number One over to a phone counselor to get the rest of his story. It wasn't pleasant.

His real name was John. Though he evaded questions that might lead to admitting murder, he acknowledged killing animals. His conversation with the counselor was disturbing and heart-breaking:

COUNSELOR: "What did you mean when you talked to Bob about tasting blood?"

JOHN: "I kill animals. Cats, dogs, squirrels. Animals like that. Then I put my hands in their blood and lick it off my hands. It gives me a high and makes me smile."

COUNSELOR: "Does anybody else know you do this?"

JOHN: "Just my six-year-old daughter. I'm teaching her to sacrifice animals and taste their blood."

INNOCENT ANIMALS

The animals John was teaching his little girl to sacrifice were once warm, furry, and cuddly. Mother Nature endowed them with the look and feel of all that humans like in an animal. Though not easily domesticated like a cat or dog, rabbits are popular as a unique pet gift, especially at Easter. The only thing rabbits don't have going for them are tear ducts. Mother Nature left those out. Zoologists don't know why. But those who administer the Draize test are grateful.

The Draize test is named for the experimenter who developed it—Dr. Draize. Since rabbits have no tear ducts to wash out harmful substances, the fuzzy creatures bear the brunt of eye irritancy tests designed to detect toxicity in cosmetics. Rabbits are restrained in stocks, and their eyes are ulcerated to test whether certain mascaras and eyeshadows are safe for human use.

Such examples of disregard for our fellow creatures have fueled the fire of animal rights activists. They cite other instances of barbarianism against innocent animals. Dogs are shot in the leg during "wound-care" experiments so military doctors can gain battlefield training by operating on open lacerations. Cats are tormented with a gas flame to gauge the effects of burns. Monkeys are subjected to psychological isolation until they eat their own infants, crushing their babies' skulls in their mouths.

Although insulin, polio vaccines, and open-heart surgery have resulted from experiments on laboratory specimens, animal rights advocates say such research has gotten out of hand, making vivisection a veritable hell on earth for innocent animals.

What is known publicly of experimental maiming of our furry friends pales when compared with the silent slaughter perpetrated by self-styled Satanists day after day. Most instances of devil worshiping animal mutilations and sacrifices are not uncovered, except when someone like Number One comes forward. Those who once participated in satanic ceremonies unhesitatingly reveal that killing animals is an integral part of appeasing dark forces.

In the mid-1970s, there were persistent reports about finding sheep, cattle, and horses whose reproductive organs had been removed and their blood drained. In the western United States from New Mexico to northern Alberta, Canada, talk of prize bulls and valued quarter horses being butchered was rampant. In 1980, *Newsweek* reported accounts of mutilated livestock in twenty-seven states.[1] The Iowa Department of Criminal Investigation (DCI) claimed to have several suspects from satanic groups. But when the DCI went to the Des Moines Public Library to consult books on Satanism, every volume on the subject had been checked out. Library officials refused to turn over the circulation records, citing a potential invasion of privacy as reason for their reluctance. The investigation apparently floundered.

Those who scoffed at the satanic mutilation theory called the idea an example of mass hysteria, akin to a witch hunt. They blamed preying animals, but their predator hypothesis couldn't explain some of the mutilations: needle marks in the animals' jugular veins, the surgical precision by which eyes and vital organs had been removed, the strange emphasis on dismembering genitals, the lack of body fluids and traces of spilled blood, the cleanly cut holes in the skull to extricate brains, and indications of burns on the hides.

Police files contain documented confessions of satanic involvement in animal mutilations. An Oklahoma woman, who spent five years in a devil worshipping cult, said she made numerous forays to remote areas where cattle were killed and their blood removed by an embalming machine. Her wealthy cult used a helicopter and several trucks to avoid detection. The helicopter would transport the cow to a remote location or a truck with a telescoping lift would hold a cult member in the air while he performed the mutilations. Veterinarians instructed cult members how to acquire the needed blood and body parts. Large animals were selected because of the huge quantities of blood required for satanic baptismal immersion.[2]

My opinion, based on years of research and countless conversations with those involved in ritualistic sacrifices, is that during the 1970s when such activity gained attention, organized occult groups were indeed involved in the ceremonial slaughter of livestock. Though some instances could be attributed to predators, other cases bore clear trademarks of black magic killings. As more became known about the mutilations, the occult groups realized they would be discovered, and, therefore, changed their ritualistic practices.

The use of cattle is particularly noteworthy. In the more advanced stages of Luciferian worship, cows play an important ritualistic role. Many groups trace their origins to ancient agrarian cults. Egyptians, Canaanites, and Babylonians had pagan religions that revered the cow as a mother goddess and combined bestiality with bovine genital veneration. Even today, tourists to the Egyptian pyramids can walk through subterranean passages and witness row upon row of elaborate stone sarcophagi used to entomb sacred cattle. The Valley of the Kings in Luxor contains five-thousand-year-old wall paintings that picture humans cohabiting with cattle and consorting sexually with other livestock.

Though organized satanic cults are a small part of the underground occult movement in America, their largely unknown presence is pervasive enough to account for the reported cases of animal mutilations. Without divulging confidences, I can reveal that I have personally counseled those who admit involvement in such cults. They are reluctant to acknowledge these crimes, fearing their stories would be discredited as outlandish fabrications of unstable minds.

CHILDREN OF THE ALTAR OF EVIL

The ceremonial use of innocent animals is tragic, but nowhere near as abhorrent as the abuse, torture, and even murder of innocent children whose parents, mentors, and abductors offer them to the devil.

Dr. Gregory Simpson, a Los Angeles pediatrician, began looking into the ritual abuse of children in 1985 after treating many scarred young patients. One dead girl's chest was carved with a pentagram. Dr. Simpson says, "The conclusion I reached is that satanic abuse of small children does exist, and it's something that needs to be dealt with by the medical community."[3]

Chicago police occult crime expert Robert Simandahl is also concerned about ritual abuse of children. He says, "It's a subject that makes street gang activity look like a nursery school rhyme."[4]

In the words of Jeffrey Burton Russell, history professor and authority on the idea of the devil in Western civilization, "The rash of appallingly degenerative crimes, including the violation of children and the mutilation of animals, can be tolerated only by a society determined to deny at any cost the radical existence of evil."[5]

THE TESTIMONY OF VICTIMS

Only recently have human victims begun to reveal unbelievable tales of terror. They say ritualized murder begins with killing small animals, then larger ones. Next comes killing isolated adults who are kidnapped at random, followed by the systematic abduction, torture, defilement, and eventual sacrifice of children.

Their incredible narratives reveal striking similarities. Boise police occult investigator, Larry Jones, says, "The statements by victims from different parts of the country tally with each other ... and it's being corroborated by therapists."[6]

Common elements combine to form a framework of evil. First a blood relative or trusted friend inducts a child. Secret ceremonies instill a ritualistic fear of evil, accompanied by robed and hooded figures, naked women on altars, hypnotic chants, goblets of animal blood, bottles of human flesh preserved in formaldehyde, and orgies between adults and children and children with animals. The eating of feces, drinking of urine, sacrifices of babies, and taking of pictures for pornographic purposes are other elements that law enforcement authorities and therapists are beginning to uncover. Some cases of cannibalism have been reported.

Women previously involved in satanic cults tell of becoming brides to Satan. Others claim they were inducted to become baby breeders, to conceive babies for sacrifice without birth or death records. In her book, *Satan's Underground*, author Lauren Stratford tells of being forced to watch the sacrifice of her own infant.[7]

Lauren is not alone. A 1988 "Geraldo" telecast featured testimony from several women who said they were kept by satanic cults to breed babies. Jacquie Balodis said she trained baby breeders, brainwashed from birth to believe such atrocities were normal. Her first two births from pregnancies induced by her stepfather were sacrificed, which she then considered an honor. Balodis now counsels other women who have been breeders and has a six-month waiting list.[8]

During the "Geraldo" telecast, a woman named Annette claimed breeders were sexually stimulated prepubescently in preparation for impregnation by age eight or nine. Gloria testified she was pregnant at ten, and the baby was sacrificed. At age eleven, she had another baby, which was sold to other cult members. In such cases, labor often was prematurely induced. A woman named Cheryl described her baby being impaled through the heart by an upside-down cross. To deal with the horror, baby breeders say they blocked out reality by multiple personalities and other forms of denial.[9]

MARKED FOR DEATH

Terrified teenagers have called "TALK-BACK" because they were marked for sacrifice at birth. One such teen was Joe, a young man who called me on a day the phone lines were opened to anyone with a question regarding the occult.

"A friend at school told me to listen to your show," Joe began. "My friend knows I play in a black metal band called Lords of Darkness. I'm sure glad I listened because I've got a big problem," he declared.

"What's that?"

"Today's the 28th, right? Well, next month, on the 8th, I have a birthday."

"Happy birthday," I congratulated him.

"You wouldn't say that if you knew what's going to happen on my birthday. I just found out myself last Saturday. I'm going to be sacrificed to Satan."

"You're what!" I exclaimed. "Who's going to do it?"

"My parents. They've been into Satan worship all my life. I never thought much about it. It's just the way I was raised, you know, like some kids are raised Baptist. For me, my parents worship Lucifer."

"Why didn't you know before that you were destined to be sacrificed?"

"The subject never came up until I went to church. Several days ago, a girl I like asked me to go to her church. When I got home, my brother told my mother where I'd been. That's when she told me I'd have to be killed."

"How old are you?"

"Fifteen. I don't want to die. But it's all there in the black box."

"What black box?" I inquired.

"My parents have this black box they keep for the devil. It has several things in it—*The Satanic Bible*, a picture of my mother, black candles, goblets, daggers, and my birth certificate. Keeping my birth certificate in that box signifies a pact that I have to die some day. Now that I've been to a Christian church, my mother's guardian spirit has told her I have to die on my next birthday."

We wasted no time getting help for Joe. He was given the phone number of "TALK-BACK"'s local radio station affiliate and subsequently visited the station where he was directed to professional counseling. Joe eventually took the black box from his home, smashed it with a hammer, and burned the contents except for his birth certificate. Then he started a new life free from his parents' satanistic practices.

The primitive idea of human sacrifice has an ignominious history. Offering human victims in propitiatory rites reverts to the Canaanites of the Middle East and the Meso-American Aztecs. The latter stained Huitzilopochtli temples with the blood of thousands of victims. The tradition is also found among ancient Greeks, Hindus, and druids. Such sacrifice was sometimes meant to atone for the wrongs of an entire group. Other times, human oblation was used to appease the gods after a natural disaster.

Human sacrifice among current satanic cults is often well organized and extremely efficient. Anticoagulants are used to store blood drained from a body, which may be disposed of in a portable crematorium. The idea of murdering another human for religious purposes is borrowed from black magic literature. Satanist Aleister Crowley, whose evil deeds will be discussed in Chapter 11, wrote: "For the highest spiritual working, one must accordingly choose that victim which contains the greatest and purest force. A male child of perfect innocence and high intelligence is the most satisfactory and suitable victim."[10]

A book called *The Black Arts* states: "When the grimoires (black magic books) talk about killing a kid, they really mean a human-child . . . there is a tradition that the most effective sacrifice to demons is the murder of a human being."[11]

MOLESTED AND MISSING CHILDREN

Some cult watchers and police agree that a large number of missing children are victims of human sacrifice cults. According to the few survivors, children are abducted and subjected to the terrifying intimidation of drugs and brainwashing before being sacrificed. They are warned that no one will believe them and that their parents will never want them back. Every technique of the cult is carefully planned to gain control of the youngsters' thoughts and behavior.

The defilement of children is important to Satanists. The more helpless the victim, the greater proof of their devotion to the devil. They also believe that the more pure the sacrifice for Satan, the more power they obtain from the god of darkness. Innocent children and guiltless babies are perfect victims. Officer Mitch White of the Beaumont, California Police Department estimates that *95 percent of all missing children are victims of occult-related abductions.*[12]

Throughout America, children are becoming victims of horrendous assaults. For instance, a thirty-seven-year-old California babysitter and her boyfriend were charged with sexual assault, lewdness with a child, and child pornography. Their victims, ages three, six, and eight, suffered nightmares, behavior disorders, and withdrawal after being held captive by Satanists, who ritualistically raped them. Naked, they were forced to watch the sacrificial slaughter of cows, horses, cats, and birds.[13]

In another reported case of ritual abuse, investigators were told that victims were forced to drink blood and eat feces. One of the children said he watched a boy named Bobby, who had lived in a cage, participate in a ceremony before he was decapitated and cannibalized by adults. Seven children were treated for depression, suicidal feelings, and regressive development.[14]

One victim of ritualistic child abuse related to me an account almost too terrible to tell. At the age of five, she was taken to the room of the dying cult leader for a sexual initiation. A painful vaginal penetration was performed with the soon-to-be-corpse to insure that his semen would be passed on ceremonially, a ritual designed to confer upon her the spirits he had conjured and served. When the leader died, she was ceremonially subjected to sadomasochistic violence too lurid to reveal. Suffice to say, her sexual organs were violated and abused in ways only a demented mind could conceive. Finally, she was forced to have anal, oral, and vaginal sex with every member of the cult, as well as several animals—all this at five years of age. To this day she remembers the orgiastic scene which followed, involving indiscriminate coupling of every sexual deviancy, including animal and human.

The ingestion of human waste products was often forced upon her. On one occasion she was buried alive for several days, breathing through a small air tube inserted into her coffin. To terrorize her further, non-poisonous snakes were placed in her burial tomb. Our conversation was the first time she had revealed what had happened to her. Why?

Suppose someone told you the story I've just related? Would you believe it? Do you believe what I've written above? Do I believe it? Yes, but I can't blame you if your credulity is stretched.

Law enforcement officials and the courts often feel the same way. In fact, the story of ritualistic abuse of children remains largely untold simply because it is so unbelievable. Satanic cults deliberately fabricate preposterous forms of child victimization, knowing that the more unthinkable their atrocity, the less likely the victim will be believed.

THE CRIME OF THE 90s

Chicago police detective Robert Simandahl calls satanic felony and murder "the crime of the 90s."[15] Young murderers like Sean Sellers are loners whose misdeeds are acts of emotionally disturbed individuals. But the most sobering menace to society comes from members of organized criminal cults controlled by adults who deliberately commit violence as part of their satanic beliefs.

A teenage "TALK-BACK" caller named Arthur claimed membership in such a cult. "I belong to LEDA," he exclaimed. "That's an acronym meaning 'The lascivious and extreme domination of animals.'"

As absurd as his story sounded, Arthur seemed serious. "We believe in the violent overthrow of all governments and in total anarchy," he said. "Then weekly human sacrifices will be established. Right now there are only 134 of us, but we are a powerful international group. Our headquarters is in Paris."

"Why did you adopt the name LEDA?" I asked.

"Because bestiality is one of our main practices. We've crucified a pig on a cross to prove our devotion to the devil."

"If you've killed animals, would you kill humans too, including children?"

"Sure, to achieve our goals. We want to go to hell. We don't believe in love."

The easiest recruits for satanic groups are runaway teenagers. Often abused, neglected, and acquainted with the consequences of evil, they feel they have nothing to lose. They adopt the attitude that evil is pervasive and triumphant, so they might as well join it. Viewing themselves as victims of a competitive world and an adversarial society, they see Satanism as a way to get what they want fast. Too late they learn that the price of getting out can be death. Some who would like to leave are presented with photographs taken of them during ceremonies, a convenient blackmailing technique.

Arthur's story may seem outrageous, but hundreds of bizarre cults operate secretly. They are different from the more visible devil worshiping cults like the Church of Satan, which repudiates all responsibility for the violation of minors.

Circumstantial evidence indicates that nationwide covens of child molesters are in touch with one another.[16] On September 27, 1987, a *Minneapolis Star Tribune* headline read, "Police Expert Warns of Satanism." The story reported that police had uncovered computer records linking child molestation rings, and that similarities of techniques used to violate the innocent indicated interaction between such groups. Investigators believe most networking is informal, extended by families and friends or from one generation to the next.

As with cocaine cartels, these satanic cults follow a hierarchial leadership. Leaders come from all walks of life, including the wealthy and influential. Victims I have counseled say one reason for their silence is that they would have to accuse powerful figures in the community whose credibility is much greater than teenagers who are caught up in such diversions as black metal music and drugs or alcohol.

Some investigators of satanic crimes suggest highly placed Satanists have even infiltrated the criminal justice system.[17] Law enforcement officials privately admit being ordered by superiors to cease investigations of satanic crimes. Others complain of political restrictions and unnecessary constraints.

The extent of the satanic crime network is difficult to estimate. One expert believes there are about sixty thousand hardcore Satanists nationwide, about a third located in California.[18] Larry Kahner, author of *Cults That Kill*, says there is evidence of nationwide connections between black magic groups and drug and pornography rings. Unfortunately, satanic crimes are often difficult to prosecute.

CRIMINAL PROSECUTION

An occult crime is often hard to detect and to prove in a court of law. There is no pattern to these crimes for detectives to follow since victims are snatched at whim. Often all evidence is destroyed when victims are either burned or their bodies cut into pieces and buried. The most paradoxical obstruction to prosecution is our nation's criminal justice system itself. Courts often refuse to handle cases in which the practice of Satanism alone is considered a sufficient criminal motive because Satanism is an officially recognized religion.

If the state does prosecute, much evidence is not admissible in court since it involves religious ceremonies. Additionally, just performing a satanic rite is insufficient cause for prosecution. Constitutional rights of religious freedoms allow Satanists free reign to worship the devil as they choose, so long as no law is violated.

Judges are reluctant to admit testimony of satanic abuse from small children in a court of law. Even in cases where medical symptoms indicate a crime has occurred, the veracity of the child's testimony is strained when he talks about being drugged and observing bloody ceremonies. The sacrifice of innocents continues because society is accustomed to Hollywood's horror genre. Thus, when a victim comes forward, especially a child, the account of abuse too closely resembles a fictional splatter-film.

WHAT YOU CAN DO TO STOP THE SLAUGHTER

Ritualistic abuse of children can be halted if concerned citizens take action. Police, social workers, therapists, and parents must be aware of the symptoms of abuse and advise children on how to avoid being vulnerable. If your child needs day care, schedule un-announced visits to the center and demand entry any time you wish. Teach your children that their bodies are their own and that no one, not even a family member or relative, has the right to touch them in a private place. Children should also be taught not to take rides, go on walks, or engage in any activity with someone they don't know, no matter how friendly and helpful the person may be. Saying "Don't take candy from strangers" isn't enough.

Consult a physician immediately if you detect unusual marks on your child's body, especially in the genital area. Be watchful for severe changes in childhood behavior surrounding sleep patterns, nightmares, toilet habits, and language. If your youngster suddenly begins using forbidden words or discusses sexual conduct in an unusually explicit manner, take special note of its cause.

Teach your child at an early age that horror movies and exploitive TV programs about the occult are off-limits because they are dangerous. Cultivate the concept of a loving, all-powerful God, not a cruel judge who sarcastically scrutinizes every action. Abductors attempt to brainwash their victims to believe that God will judge them for what they've engaged in so there is no point in trying to escape.

A NEW NUMBER ONE

John's conversation with our phone counselor lasted a half hour, as she talked to him about his involvement in Satanism. Like most Satanists, John had never known love. His childhood was a nightmare of neglect and abuse.

"When I was three years old, my mother held my hand on a hot frying pan to punish me," John told the counselor. "But that wasn't the worst thing she did. Not only was I beaten unconscious several times, once she stabbed me with a knife."

Carefully, the counselor explained that John must not allow his mother's mental instability to become his problem. His mother's cruelty was outrageous, obviously, but to continue her dysfunctional patterns in his life could only prolong his victimization.

The counselor read from the Bible how Christ was mistreated at the hands of those who should have responded favorably to His message of love. "God understands your pain," the counselor said. "He too suffered unjustly. But the message He gave us is that returning love for hate is the pathway to forgiveness and inner healing."

After talking to our phone counselor, John remembered a Bible a friend had given him seven years earlier. He opened its pages and began to understand that love was a more powerful lure than the enticement of evil.

The more he read and the more he talked to our counselors, the more he began to see how deviant his behavior had become. John's life was changed, and so was his daughter's. He explained to her how wrong his actions had been. He told her what he was learning about God's love. That time of reading and reflection was the beginning of a miraculous change in John's life. Today, he is a Christian street minister and reaches out with compassion to others who were victimized as he was.

"God is now Number One in my life," John declared in a follow-up call to my audience.

At "TALK-BACK," we find that our best approach to combating satanistic beliefs is by presenting biblical truth. Confidence in the devil can be resisted only by a belief in God. In the next part of this book, we will look at the beliefs of Satanists—the organized churches of Satan; the philosophy of Aleister Crowley, which inspires so many black metal rock groups; the old black magic of witchcraft; and satanic folk religions.

Though John's story is dramatic, I wonder how many other Number Ones need help? How many more unknown victims of ritualistic abuse silently suffer, biding their time until something clicks inside their heads and they gain the upper hand, turning from victim to perpetrator? Unless the sacrifice of innocents is stopped, society's future will be sacrificed on the altar of rampant victimization.

PART FOUR

The Roots of Satanism

10

Mephistopheles' Manifesto

"I'm a Satanist. I hurt people. I destroy them."

Kay wasn't the first seventeen-year-old to call my talk show and say something like that. But the conversation took a strange twist almost immediately.

"Did you get the letter I wrote you?" she asked. "The one with the blood on it?"

The letter had arrived the day before. I asked a staff member to fetch it from my office. In the meantime I stalled.

"Who told you to call?" I inquired, totally unprepared for Kay's incredible answer.

"The spirits I conjure. One's name is Hate. The other is Lies. Anyway, I listen to you a lot. You're funny. The best comedy hour of the day!"

My secretary put Kay's letter in front of me.

"Your letter has an upside-down cross on the envelope. Inside it says, 'Satan rules!' You've drawn knives on it. They look like they're dripping in blood . . . Wait a minute! This looks like real blood . . . Is it?"

"Yeah," Kay confidently exclaimed. "My blood. I cut myself in a ceremony just for you."

"Since the audience doesn't know what's in this letter, let me read it to them. It's a prayer to Satan: 'You're wonderful. You offer me so much. I want you to come into my heart. I need you. I will serve you. Take control of my life.'

"You've signed it, 'Yours truly, Lucifer.' Did you write this by yourself?" I inquired.

"With a little help from Lies and Hate."

"I suppose they helped you write the P.S.: 'If you don't devote yourself to Satan, watch out. This is not an empty threat but . . .'"

Kay interrupted. " . . . but rather a promise."

"You still remember the words?"

"I wrote them, didn't I? I meant it too."

Many teenagers are as ardent as Kay in their dedication to the devil and his lies. To understand why, we must probe the cultural seeds of Satanism planted by occult religious movements. These sects extoll the doctrines of hate that appeal to neglected and confused youth. The most basic question to be weighed in this section is a fundamental consideration of theology: Is the devil real? Is he a mythical monster? Or is he, as Carl Jung believed, an archetypal image of evil?

Does Satan really exist? John Wesley, the founder of Methodism, answered "Yes!" to that question. "There is no evil done or spoken or thought without the assistance of the devil, who worketh with strong though secret power. All the works of evil nature are the work of the devil," he said.

Many today, including some in the clergy, don't agree. They say that belief in a personal devil is a medieval fantasy constructed to anthropomorphically describe evil's existence. Society at large and youths in particular are desensitized to the authenticity of evil. Few realize an intense, intangible, spiritual struggle is taking place every day.

In his book, *People of the Lie,* psychiatrist M. Scott Peck chronicles his pilgrimage from a skeptic who did not believe the devil exists to an active participant in exorcisms. Peck writes, "The spirit I witnessed at each exorcism was clearly, utterly, and totally dedicated to opposing human life and growth. It told both patients to kill themselves."[1] He concludes, "I know no more accurate epithet for Satan than the Father of Lies."[2]

Unfortunately such absolute assurance concerning Satan and the reality of contact with the spirit world is not shared by the average American. One theologian has observed that the devil's cleverest wile is to convince humans he doesn't exist.

But the Bible strongly counters that assumption. Its pages are filled with references to Lucifer as a murderer, liar, adversary, and destroyer. He is alluded to as Beelzebub, Apollyon, and Mammon.

He is described as being an angel of light when it suits his purpose, and a slanderer and tempter when that is convenient. For some, he is the ultimate cop-out to evade human responsibility for misconduct, as expressed in the quip, "The devil made me do it."

Biblical Proof

Millions of devout Christians believe the Bible teaches Satan is alive and well and in a continual struggle with God for men's souls. The prophet Ezekiel speaks of the devil as an exceedingly beautiful angel living in the presence of God.[3] The prophet Isaiah indicates that Lucifer's sin, which led him to be expelled from heaven, was the arrogant assumption that he could exalt himself to equality with God.[4]

In the book of Job we see Satan appearing before God's throne, requesting permission to tempt God's choicest servant.[5] The battle continues in the New Testament where Jesus was tempted by Satan who offered Christ all the kingdoms of this world.[6] Satan also suggested that Jesus throw himself from the pinnacle of the temple to be delivered by God's angels.[7] Such a publicity stunt could have convinced millions Jesus was the Messiah. But Christ understood Satan's motives, as too few today discern, and didn't yield to the trap set for him.

What is the historic Christian position concerning Satan? He's described in Scripture as a wicked being who tempts and deceives. He possesses the power to perform miracles, a feat to be displayed at the end of this age when his puppet, the Antichrist, will rule the world. The Bible warns Christians to be aware of his evil devices[8] and admonishes disciples of Jesus to avoid being taken captive by the devil's snares.[9] As a seducer, Satan is seen in Eden's Garden luring Adam and Eve into forbidden conduct,[10] which leads to their spiritual death.[11] Christians are also promised that the devil's domain is limited, and that Christ defeated the devil's hold on death through his resurrection.[12] One day, sin, rebellion, darkness, wickedness, deception, and murder—all deeds of the devil—will be abolished.[13]

THE SATAN TEENS WORSHIP

The biblical portrait of evil is much different from the perception of Satan held by contemporary teens. The young Satanists I confront on my radio show think of Lucifer as an adolescent chum who offers devilish delights. Hell is an eternal pleasure palace of endless orgasms. Evil is an impish indulgence met with a mischievous wink instead of divine disapproval. Above all, they see Satan as someone who cares more about them than God or their parents, since he offers uninhibited gratification in place of sober moderation.

To teenage Satanists, the devil is a friend who offers money, drugs, sex, excitement, and whatever their selfish desires fancy. When parents and society say no, the devil says yes. When God says "Wait," Satan says, "You can have it all, right now!"

Raised in an instant-everything society, teenagers think the devil delivers "microwavable" malevolence, quick fixes for long-term ills, and immediate satisfaction instead of delayed fulfillment. The seventies Rolling Stones' anthem, "You Can't Always Get What You Want," seems passé to youth facing the nineties. Madison Avenue has led them to believe their every whim deserves fulfillment, and worshiping the devil is a shortcut to gratifying every immoral instinct.

In an age of organized rebellion, Satanism champions a creed of self-centeredness. For thirty years, self-improvement books and motivational seminars have emphasized looking out for number one. Although muted, the underlying supposition of human potential courses has been "me first." Satanism condones such human frailties. Lying, cheating, gluttony, and greed are acceptable if they bring satisfaction. After all, the ultimate design of Satanists is to become godlings, deities with all of Lucifer's passions and pursuits.

Another lure is the search for a non-narcotic high. Satanists experience the raw essence of evil by participating in sacrificial ceremonies that seem to induce altered states of consciousness not unlike the psychoactive influence of hallucinogens. Also, in many solitary satanic cults, drugs play an important part in the ceremonies. In teenage cults, drugs and alcohol are integral.

LITERATURE OF THE LIE

Aiding the cultural climate of occult acceptance is a flourishing body of literature that exploits the darker side of human nature and the excesses of evil. Clive Barker, an English writer, remembers watching the murder scene of Hitchcock's thriller "Psycho" at fifteen years of age and says, "I thought I'd love to do this to people (scare them). This is such a nice thing to do to people." Of his six books, which feature man-eating pigs and monstrous subway murderers, Barker says, "I always used to side with the demons. I never used to care two hoots about the hero. I was interested in the dark, mysterious creatures the hero faces."[14]

As any aficionado of horror knows, author Stephen King is the master of dread and death. From *Dead Zone* and *Carrie* to *It* and *Pet Sematary*, King has sold more than sixty million books. His plots feature clairvoyance, hauntings, psychic powers, vampires, poltergeists, and assorted psychopaths. King explains his fascination with these topics by saying, "There is a part of us that needs to vicariously exorcise the darker side of our feelings."[15] Barker and King are using satanic phenomena to sell fiction. They're not all that different from the black metal stars whose ultimate goal is wealth, not devil worship.

GRIMOIRES: BLACK MAGICK TEXTBOOKS

Grimoires, black magic textbooks for evoking demons, are the real thing. They are non-fiction, how-to books for the apprentice Satanist. These manuals of magic have been ascribed to Solomon, Albertus Magnus, and assorted wizards. They describe rituals, ceremonies, and miscellaneous occult practices. Among the most notable are: *Liber Spiritum; Shemamphoras* (a Hebrew book); *Oupnekhat* (a Sanskrit manual); *Hell's Coercion* (attributed to Johannes Faustus); *The Key of Solomon* (ascribed to King Solomon); and *The Lesser Key of Solomon* (explaining the demonic hierarchy).[16]

The Key of Solomon *and* The Book of Enoch

The Key of Solomon is the most famous book of antiquity extolling demonism. The Jewish historian Josephus in the first century A.D. referred to an occult book, supposedly written by King Solomon, with explicit instructions for incantations. This manual for summoning evil spirits was said to be composed by devils themselves. French and Latin versions abounded in the eighteenth century. The most popular version today was edited and embellished by Aleister Crowley.

The Book of Enoch is an apocryphal work attributed to the biblical Enoch, composed in the second century, B.C. It is based on an unorthodox interpretation of Genesis 6:4. "The sons of God came in to the daughters of men and they bore children to them."

The Book of Enoch claims these "sons of Gods" were fallen angels who taught the powers of witchcraft to the beautiful women they seduced. Included in Enoch's book are the names of rebellious angels (demons) whose mission it is to torture mankind.

The Necronomicon

The two most popular books representing the Satanist genre are *The Satanic Bible* (discussed in Chapter 8) and *The Necronomicon*. The latter was the invention of American occult and horror-fiction author Howard Phillips Lovecraft (1890–1937). Lovecraft developed a mythology around the "dread Cthulhu," in which powers of evil and darkness from another time and space threatened to control the world. *The Necronomicon*, the Book of Dead Names, was their legendary occult text. Lovecraft claimed it was compiled by the "mad Arab Abdul Alhazred." In fact, the whole thing was concocted by Lovecraft, who cited references to it in his other stories.

A group of writers and researchers, headed by occult scholar Colin Wilson, collaborated to present *The Necronomicon: The Book of Dead Names* as a newly discovered masterpiece of occult literature. Wilson attempted to suggest that Lovecraft's invention may have had a historical basis in fact. Various occultists have claimed that a similar work has existed for centuries, rooted in *The Book of the Essence of the Soul* by an Arabian mystic name Alkindi. Others say the *Necronomicon* was truly based on *Al Asiz*, an ancient Arabic book on demons.[17]

The popular edition of the *Necronomicon* contains a dedication to Aleister Crowley. Credit is also given to "the demon PERDURABO" (a name Crowley assumed). The preface ends with the appeal, "We enter the New Age of the Crowned and Conquering Child, Horus, not in a slouch toward Bethlehem, born within us at the moment we conquer the lurking fear in our souls."[18]

The *Necronomicon* is frequently quoted by teenage Satanists who call "TALK-BACK." Though they usually know little of its origins, the book's evil fascinates them. Reversing the biblical account of Lucifer's rebellion against god, the *Necronomicon* says the devil, the horned deity, SIN, was supreme among the Body of the Ancient

Ones.[19] The book warns that using its incantations, supposedly the oldest in occult history, may arouse demons that have not been summoned in six thousand years. Once called forth, the admonition declares, "Ordinary exorcism and banishing formulae have thus far proved extremely inadequate by experienced magicians."[20]

In addition to an introduction and conclusion by the "mad Arab," the *Necronomicon* is divided into sections of line drawings of amulets and invocations. These are supposedly derived from the ancient Sumerians, a once-flourishing pagan culture in Mesopotamia, the site of Babylonia as well as Abraham's Ur of the Chaldees. Sumeria was ruled by seven cities, each with a different deity. The Sumerian civilization has been closely aligned with Aryan ideology, and their language resembles Hindu Sanskrit. Their religion was a complex system of ritual magic, including the summoning of evil powers.

Many of the amulets and invocations are in what is said to be the original Sumerian language. Some rituals, such as the Conjuration of the Watcher, require a preliminary sacrifice "in a clean and new bowl," though the nature of the "sacrifice" is not specified.[21] *The Necronomicon* concludes with the statement, "This is the book of the Servants of the Gods."[22]

Apart from its blasphemies and admitted "abominations," the *Necronomicon* is a primer for introducing students of the black arts to the methods of summoning the most foul spirits to accomplish evil bidding. Teenagers like Sean Sellers, and Kay, who wrote me the blood-stained letters, undoubtedly overlook the possibly fictionalized origins of the book and take its invocations of evil seriously.

SATANIC GROUPS

Adherents of Satanism fall into two general categories. First are the psychotically and criminally inclined groups who appear to operate without external jurisdiction. These are the solitary Satanists, like Sean Sellers, who are usually responsible for grave-robbings, animal sacrifices, body mutilations, sexual orgies, church vandalizing, and blood ceremonies. They are more likely to have informal, evolving beliefs. Most teenagers involved in Satanism are attracted to this form of devil worship.

The second category is the organized institution of Satanism, represented by the Church of Satan. Its philosophy centers on the ritualized catharsis of venting negative emotions to justify uninhibited conduct. Satanism is a religion that strikes back instead of turning the other cheek. Both self-styled and institutional groups use rituals to express their contempt for Christianity.

THE BLACK MASS

The best-known ritual is the black mass, which evolved during the Middle Ages as a parody of the Christian mass. A Mendes goat symbol or obscene figure of Christ is placed on the altar. Black candles are burned, and the chalice is filled with blood. A nude woman serves as the altar with the mass being celebrated on her buttocks or stomach. The host is desecrated, and backwards prayers are offered. Traditionally the celebrants are nude except for robes adorned with satanic symbols. When a human sacrifice is offered, the blood of the sacrificial child is mixed with the chalice's contents and offered to the devil.

Most teenagers don't participate in such ceremonies, since they prefer the spontaneity of self-styled ritualism as opposed to more formal adulation of Lucifer. Instead, teen Satanists make up their own protocol of evil with only a general outline to guide them. Ceremonialism is usually not a high priority for informal occult groups. The intent of unaligned Satanists is generally to provide an excuse to indulge in criminal and morally debasing conduct. Conversely, organized Satanists have as their ultimate aim the restoration of Lucifer to a position they believe is his rightful place as ruler of the universe.

The devil is the defeated foe of God, but as far as many frail humans are concerned, his strategy seems to be working. The modern era of his reign was heralded on June 19, 1972, when the face of a hooded symbol of Satan glared from the cover of *Time* magazine with the headline: "THE OCCULT REVIVAL—Satan Returns."

THE CHURCH OF SATAN

The author of *The Satanic Bible* and founder of the Church of Satan, Anton LaVey, is the father of contemporary Satanism in America. A former animal trainer and carnival employee, LaVey gained a reputation as an expert in hypnotism and mentalism. On

April 30, 1966, the occult holiday of Walpurgisnacht (the witches sabbat announcing the transition from winter to spring), LaVey shaved his head and announced the formation of the Magic Circle, a secret ritualistic group from which he eventually organized The Church of Satan. Based on the disillusionment of his carnival years, LaVey, the "black pope of Satanism," declared, "Since worship of fleshly things produces pleasure, there would then be a temple of glorious indulgence."

LaVey studied the occult assiduously and began holding regular meetings to present his ideas about vampires, witchcraft, and sex. He gained national press by performing a satanic baptism on his three-year-old daughter and conducting the funeral for a sailor member. Celebrities started showing up, including Sammy Davis, Jr., who wore a satanic medallion around his neck. LaVey claimed that actresses Jayne Mansfield and Marilyn Monroe were among his sex partners.

LaVey's brand of Satanism was more theater than substance. He emphasized the drama of his ceremonies and disappointed those who expected membership in the Church of Satan to be a one-way ticket to orgiastic frenzy. True, there was a nude on the altar, but that, too, was show biz. As LaVey told everyone all along, there really isn't a devil. Lucifer is only a metaphor for man's dark inner desires.

Church of Satan teachings resemble an indulgent form of psychotherapy more than any religious commitment to evil. To LaVey, man's true enemy is guilt, instilled by Christianity, and the path to individual freedom is through pursuing sin on a regular basis. LaVey admits he regards nothing as supernatural and leans toward the Aleister Crowley school of magic, which is based on a scientific approach to the paranormal (see Chapter 11). Drawing members from various occult groups, the Church of Satan experienced rapid growth throughout the seventies with grottos (local chapters) located in all major cities of the United States.

Today, between ten and twenty thousand adherents claim to affiliate with the Church of Satan. Worship is led by a priest who is adept in performing rituals. The highest holiday is one's birthday. After that, Walpurgisnacht (April 30) and Halloween are the most important. In addition to the books of LaVey, members are encouraged to read the writings of Ayn Rand, Friedrich Nietzsche, and

Machiavelli because of the emphasis these authors put upon excelling through human potential. Three basic kinds of rituals are performed:

- Sexual rituals to satisfy eroticism.
- Compassionate rituals to help someone.
- Destructive rituals to get revenge.[23]

Soon rival organizations began springing up, including the Church of Satanic Brotherhood, the Order of the Black Ram, the Ordo Templi Santanas, and the Temple of Set, which was founded by former LaVey follower Michael Aquino. Some followers exploited the totalitarian aspects of Church of Satan ideology and affiliated with extremist political groups. Eventually, LaVey closed down the grottos and went into seclusion. His wife continued operating the church, and his older daughter, Karla, took on the role of spokesperson, a function more lately filled by his youngest daughter, Zena.

Today, nearing sixty, Anton LaVey still works to preserve his evil reputation for posterity, but has little to do with Church of Satan activities. His newsletter, *The Cloven Hoof*, is still circulated.

The Church of Satan has little direct influence on current Satanism as practiced among youths. Most teenagers never affiliate with LaVey unless their parents have been members, but they are heavily swayed by the rituals and beliefs set forth in *The Satanic Bible*. To teenage Satanists, Anton LaVey is an unkindly grandfather of devil worship who paved the way for the present occult explosion. Church of Satan theology is integral to teen ideas about the devil, although most youths consider organized Satanism too restrictive and outdated.*

THE TEMPLE OF SET

The most active offshoot of the Church of Satan is Dr. Michael Aquino's Temple of Set. Taking the name of his organization from the Egyptian mythological god of death, Aquino is a highly visible spokesperson for Satanism. Whereas LaVey avoids the public spot-

---

*For the most recent information regarding the Church of Satan, Arthur Lyons' book *Satan Wants You* provides an excellent secular perspective on the church, its history, and current status.[24]

light, Aquino frequents TV talk shows in the company of his wife and accomplice, Lilith Sinclair (Pat Wise). Aquino, a lieutenant colonel in the Army Reserve with top secret security clearance, specialized in psychological warfare, an expertise that probably serves him well as a Satanist. At one time a trusted ally of LaVey, Aquino was asked to organize special rituals for the Church of Satan.

Aquino claims Satan appeared to him as Set on June 21, 1975. Set, according to Aquino, was the spirit Aiwaz, who appeared to Aleister Crowley. Now, Set is inaugurating his own aeon, a time of satanic, spiritual, and intellectual enlightenment. Aquino has plucked his bushy eyebrows to form an evil stare and tattooed the number 666 on his head. That self-designation as the Antichrist claims the same identification as Aleister Crowley and picks up where the British Satanist left off.

Whereas LaVey played the role of a huckster, disclaiming all affiliation with a literal devil, Michael Aquino takes Satan much more seriously. Sounding like a cross between a Scientologist and a disciple of Werner Erhard, Aquino teaches that Setians may become gods through a process known as Xepering (pronounced Kepering or Kheffering from the Egyptian hieroglyphics for "to come into being"), a striving toward knowledge. More of an intellectual than LaVey, Aquino attracts an upwardly mobile constituency, many of them coming from backgrounds of witchcraft and Christianity. Fortunately, few teenagers actively follow Aquino; however, his high public profile lends credibility to Satanism and indirectly affects teens interested in devil worship.

As of the writing of this book, the future of the Temple of Set is uncertain. Clouding its image are charges that the Second Beast of Revelation (Aquino) was involved in a child molestation incident at the day care center of the Presidio Army Base. According to authorities, a child said she recognized Aquino as the man who molested her in a room with black walls. The little girl also claimed to recognize Aquino's wife, Lilith.[25] Aquino denies the charges, but does admit he jokingly considers himself the Antichrist and head of an elite group of magicians who will survive a coming apocalypse.

THE PROCESS CHURCH

The theology of the Process Church has apparently influenced satanic killers, most notably David Berkowitz, the convicted Son of

Sam serial murderer. Berkowitz was found guilty of six murders and seven shootings in the New York Queens and Bronx suburbs and is currently serving 365 years in prison for those crimes.

On Berkowitz's copy of *The Anatomy of Witchcraft*, he high-lighted a section on the Process Church which stated, "Thou shalt kill. They say they are dedicated to bringing about the end of the world by murder, violence and chaos—but they, the chosen, will survive to build a new world of satanic glory."[26]

Maury Terry, author of *The Ultimate Evil*, emphasizes the occult crime role of the Process Church, also known as The Foundation Faith of the Millennium. Church founder Robert DeGrimston taught a convoluted gospel claiming that Christ and Satan have de-stroyed their enmity and come together for the end of the world. Consequently, worshiping Satan is the same as worshiping Christ, and to kill for the devil is divine. Black is the favorite color of Pro-cess members, whose regalia includes black capes, inverted swasti-kas, and pentagrams. According to Maury Terry, Charles Manson was also heavily influenced by Processian philosophy. Like others who swallowed DeGrimston's teachings, Manson believed it was his duty to hasten Armageddon by confusion, murder, and death.

SPIRITUAL WARFARE ON THE HOME FRONT

"I've sold my soul to the devil," many teens phoning "TALK-BACK" tell me.

Though many teenagers take Satan seriously, their parents often scoff at the idea of the devil. They consider him either an imp with a forked tail or a myth of mystics and cartoonists. Consequently, few parents realize they are involved in spiritual warfare for the soul of their child. Such a conclusion may be a comforting denial, but it is a dangerous escape from reality.

From his Death Row jail cell, Sean Sellers speaks forcibly about the devil's deception. I asked him what he says to teens who have sold their souls to the devil.

SEAN SELLERS' ADVICE

"I tell them the devil makes you do things that are alien to your nature," Sean said. "I was a sensitive kid who wrote music and poetry. I was a good student and an athlete. I loved nature and life and wanted to be a veterinarian. But Satan changed all that.

"The devil isn't for you, he's against you. Serving Satan sounds good at first. You can have anything you want. But in the end it's horrible. Satanists think they're looking forward to having fun in hell, but the devil makes a shambles of their lives before they get there. They end up in hell on earth!"

Sean described vividly the final effects of Satanism that caused him to kill. "It took away the love for my parents and my girlfriend," he explained. "Eventually, I had no love. No mercy. No conscience. It was subtle. It happened little by little."

"What should parents do if they discover their child is interested in the occult?" I asked Sean.

"Don't panic," he advised. "That will turn them off. Find out if they've gotten occult paraphernalia out of curiosity or more serious reasons. If they're just experimenting, explain how dangerous it can be. Let them know it will destroy their lives."

"What if it's gone beyond that? Suppose a teenager is seriously involved in Satanism?"

"First look for some hard evidence like scars, tattoos, demonic drawings, and satanic paraphernalia like bones and pentagrams," Sean counseled. "If you find that stuff, don't ignore it. It gets serious quickly. Get someone who can help you.

"If your child is involved because he isn't getting attention, start paying attention. Let your child know you love him." Sean went on, "Then start putting some limits on his behavior, who he goes out with, and where he goes. That may seem harsh and cause some rebellion at first, but you've got to do it. If you don't, the outcome could be worse. Just look at me."

"What's it like on Death Row?" I asked Sean.

"My cell is seventeen feet long. It's got a desk, sink, toilet, a barred window, and a barred door," he answered. "The phone is in my cell but the cord is strung down the hallway to an outlet. Right now, I'm talking to you from inside my cell. Once a day they let me out into the yard for an hour. The rest of the time I'm behind bars."

I still didn't fully comprehend why Sean Sellers had killed so brutally at fifteen years of age, so I questioned him further. "I understand that you've become a Christian. What's the difference between what you are now and what you were?" I asked.

"Well," Sean started, "I used to believe like most Satanists that Satan is good and God is bad. I felt that Satan cared about all mankind. I loved Satan. I wanted to serve him. But after what's happened to me, I know Satan wants only to destroy mankind."

"Does Satanism give you the right to get even with anyone you want?"

"It's the opposite of the Golden Rule," Sean responded. "I believed that if someone hurts you, you hurt them back. Satanism taught me that kindness is due to those who deserve it, instead of wasting love on ingrates. You should love only those who are deserving of love."

During Sean's trial he was silent, claiming he could not recall the crime. After the verdict, Sean's memory of much of the incident returned, a fact that clouds his days with inconceivable guilt. But Sean Sellers knows now beyond any doubts why he did what he did.

"Satan will never take anything you don't give him," Sean admits. "And I gave him everything. If I hadn't gotten into Satanism, I would not be here today. Anyone who plays games with the devil is going to lose. The devil is going to use you and then throw you away."

Sean concluded with a lesson for parents learned from his own life. "After Satanism affected me I couldn't go back to what I was before."

All that changed one day in March 1986 when Sean was in the Oklahoma City county jail two weeks after the murders. Free from drugs, Sean finally felt guilty about what he had done. Someone (to this day he doesn't remember who) handed him a Bible. He opened it and began to read. Verses on love and forgiveness seemed to be on every page he turned to.

God might even forgive me, he realized. He fell to his knees, sobbing. He asked God to forgive him and to come into his heart and change his life.

When the Last Days Ministries came to the prison to lead a chapel service, a chaplain stopped by to see Sean. Every Tuesday Sean continues to meet with a group for prayer and Bible study.

"I've learned," Sean says, "that once the devil changes you, only

God can restore you. Only He can reach into a heart the occult has destroyed."

LESSONS FROM KAY'S CONCLUSION

Kay, whose story started this chapter, needed love just as Sean Sellers did. I finally interrupted her diatribe of threats and bravado, and addressed the real reason she called.

"Kay, down inside you don't want to serve Satan. But you're so hurt, confused, and mixed-up you hate yourself. You feel a sense of rejection and lack of love in your life. You've reached out to Satanism to find some kind of meaning in your life."

"Did you take psychology or what? I mean, you hit that right on the head," she responded.

"Kay," I declared, "the promises of evil are always the same—riches, love, satisfaction, power. But the devil can't deliver any of them except for a short time."

After her braggadocio attitude at the beginning of the conversation, Kay was strangely silent. In spite of her acclamations of evil, I sensed she was lonely and hurting, wishing someone would debunk her defense of the devil.

"I know why you called today. It's because you really feel bad about writing that letter with the threats and curses."

"You're right."

"And you hoped that I'd pin you down so you'd have an opportunity to face the evil in your life and let God's love forgive you for worshiping Satan."

"What can I say? I'm sorry I wrote that letter."

"I accept your apology. But you know who you really need to apologize to?"

"Yeah."

"Who?"

"You're going to say, 'God.'"

"Well, apologize to Him."

"How will I know if He's going to listen?"

"Kay, if Hate heard when you called, I know God will heed your cry of pain and regret."

I still have the blood stained letter Kay sent me nearly two years ago. But in my collection of mementos from this hurting teenager I have some other more meaningful things. Items of handiwork she took time to fashion with her own hands as a labor of love: silk tulips, a red-painted heart saying "I love you," a small, wicker basket of beaded flowers, and a picture of Kay in her high school graduation gown, an accomplishment no one thought she'd achieve. Today Kay is a student at a major Christian college.

Kay may seem like a miracle. But all it takes to reach teens like Kay is someone to look beyond "Hate" and "Lies" to see the real reason they've exchanged charity for malice and truth for deception.

Aleister Crowley's Creed

Occasionally, I receive a written challenge from a Satanist. Such was the case with Curtis McQuirt. By flattering me as a broadcaster and simultaneously insinuating that I was incapable of combating his satanic beliefs, he extended an invitation I couldn't refuse.

"Your grasp of culture, your ability to sound articulate, your impeccable command of rhetoric, and ability to talk on your feet, shifting from one logical premise to another to dazzle your multifaceted audience are outstanding. Bob, I admire your act. I come against you as a student of the Great White Brotherhood. You can go back to picking on wimpy pagans or crack-brained Satanists, or you can meet the great wild beast, me, Curtis McQuirt."

After reading Curtis's letter, I turned to my guest coordinator and said, "I accept this guy's challenge. See if you can get him on the show."

Several weeks later, I punched the button on our studio board marked GUEST. Curtis was on the line and on the air. The topic was Crowleyism.

"Do what thou wilt shall be the whole of the law," was his opening salvo, the edict of the infamous Aleister Crowley.

"Now that I've said that," Curtis explained, "there are some things I want to make clear. Bob, though you may call me a Satanist, I'm not. I don't believe in the devil except as a symbol of raw creative impulses. I am a Fellowlight."

149

"But your late mentor, Crowley, was a Satanist," I asserted. "He believed he was the Beast of the Bible's Revelation."

"Yes, but he wasn't a Satanist." Curtis responded. "He didn't believe in the devil. And he had contempt for Ouija boards, seances, table-tapping, and trance mediums. He called it 'indiscriminate necromancy by amateurs.'"

"What paranormal powers do you contact?" I asked.

"Powers within me that are part of god."

"But Jesus said that the heart of man is evil and filled with murder, fornication, covetousness, and pride,'" I answered, quoting the Bible as I often do to counteract satanic beliefs.

"What Jesus, Bob? I can list you fifteen different religious figures who were all born of virgins and came back from the dead. Like Krishna, Jesus of the druids, Quetzecoatal . . ."

"Wait a minute," I interrupted, "you're not going to compare Jesus Christ with Quetzecoatal, the feathered serpent of human-sacrificing Meso-Americans?"

"Bob, your God has the manners and morals of a spoiled child. As a Crowleyite, I am the true Christian and you are a perversion of Christianity!"

"That's preposterous, Curtis. You're the one practicing black magic. After all, Crowley was kicked out of Italy for allegedly practicing infant sacrifice. And one of his disciples there died from drinking blood."

"Yes, but he was never indicted for the supposed crimes."

"How did Crowley end up? A drug fiend. A heroin addict and a blithering idiot," I pointed out.

Since Curtis couldn't repudiate these facts, he did what most cornered debaters do; he changed the subject.

"The trouble with your kind of so-called Christianity is that you need some big daddy figure breathing down your neck, pointing life out for you step by step," Curtis asserted.

"You're wrong. The Bible tells us God loved the world and sent His Son to die for our sins."

"That's a protection racket, Bob. If God made the rules, why should He expect us to be grateful?"

The question was ludicrous. Curtis was trying to bait me, and I wouldn't bite. So I changed the subject.

"What about Crowley's bisexualism?"

"Everyone should follow their own true will. Bob, if you tell your fellow human beings what's right and what's wrong, you're trying to interfere with their wills. You're a hideous blasphemer of Christianity."

Confused? You should be! Welcome to the world of occult ideology and satanic revisionism, where black is white and wrong is right. The world of Crowleyism, thelemic magic, wiccan worship, and assorted examples of occult black magic and sinister Satanism. The world of teenagers trapped in the occult. Today's teenage Satanists are heavily influenced by Crowley's creeds, and their parents must learn the sinister roots of these diabolical doctrines.

THE CRUCIBLE OF CROWLEYISM

Born in England in 1875, Aleister Crowley became the most infamous black magician of all time. As a child he was so evil his Christian mother nicknamed him "The Beast," after Revelation's beast that came out of the sea with horns on its head, blaspheming God.[2] Ironically, Crowley's father traveled the English countryside preaching the Christian doctrines of a strict fundamentalist group known as Plymouth Brethren.

Crowley believed quite literally that he was the Beast of Revelation and declared open revolt against God. His writings, such as *Confessions* and *Magic in Theory and Practice*, stated his mission in life was to destroy Christianity and build the religion of Thelema (ritual magic based on the Greek word for "will") in its place.

Crowley was active in the Hermetic Order of the Golden Dawn, an English magical society he joined in 1898. The Order taught how to consecrate talismans, set up magic circles, travel astrally, and study esoteric mysticism known as the Cabala (also Kabbala, Hebrew occultism based on numerological interpretations of Jewish scriptures). Like occult Cabalists, Golden Dawn members believed they had power over demons through esoteric magical formulas. Members also believed they were governed by superior intelligences called Secret Chiefs. Crowley took the magical title of Perdurabo ("I will endure to the end"). He was eventually expelled from the Hermetic Order after gaining a reputation for breaking every moral law—from fornication to murder.

As a young man of twenty-eight, Crowley visited Cairo, Egypt.

There a spirit appeared to him, which he referred to as his holy guardian angel, Aiwaz. The entity Aiwaz described himself as a representative of a Great White Brotherhood of ascended spiritual entities who ruled the earth. Aiwaz told Crowley a new eon was beginning that would last two thousand years. It would be founded on occultism.

Crowley's teachings were summed up in his Law of Thelema: "This Book lays down a simple Code of Conduct. / Do what thou wilt shall be whole of the Law. / Love is the law, love under will. / There is no law beyond Do what thou wilt."[3]

Crowley's philosophy was expounded in *The Book of the Law*, which taught that history can be divided into two eras. The first was the eon of Isis, the Egyptian nature goddess, wife and sister of Osiris. During this time period, prior to 500 B.C., matriarchy and Egyptian mythology dominated humanity. The second epoch was Osiris, based on the Egyptian god of the underworld. During this time, co-inciding with the period of Judaism, Buddhism, Islam, and Christianity, man dominated. In 1904, however, humanity supposedly entered the eon of Horus, the Egyptian child-god of light, the son of Osiris and Isis. During this time, the true self of man would dominate, rather than any allegiance to external authorities, priests, or gods.

Crowley's creed was simple: "Be strong, O man! Lust! Enjoy all the things of sense. Fear not that any god shall deny thee for this." He lived what he preached. Crowley was accused of being a homosexual, a child molester, and a deviant of every sexual variation known to man. He borrowed the idea of sexual magic from Hindu tantric yoga and taught that sexual union reached its highest realm when the mind, the breath, and the semen were held still.

In Great Britain, Aleister Crowley became the head of a secret occult order based on thelemic black magic known as Argenteum Astrum (the Silver Star), the Inner Order of the Great White Brotherhood. Every member was required to go through a standardized test whereby he was supposed to interpret an unknown and unintelligible symbol through a vision or astral journey. If he passed, the candidate became a Probationer. A year later, all orders being kept, the inductee could graduate to Neophyte, acquiring control of his "body of light." The final state was that of a Zelator. In the 1920s and 1930s, Crowley accomplished with Satanism in England what Anton LaVey did for devil worship in America in the 1960s.

During the first World War, Crowley transferred his activities to America. The press proclaimed him "the wickedest man in the world." He also spent time in Italy, but was expelled because Italian authorities accused his disciples of sacrificing human infants in occult rituals. According to one source, Crowley resided in the Abbey of Thelema near Cefalu, Sicily, and revived ancient Dionysian ceremonies. During a 1921 ritual, he induced a he-goat to copulate with his mistress, then slit the animal's throat at the moment of orgasm.[4]

Crowley insisted that divination be as precise as "scientific thesis," and declared that invoking spirits should not be a subjective phenomenon, but be accompanied by smells and visible forms. He dedicated his life to rescuing the occult from the "ill repute which . . . has made it an object of aversion to those very minds whose enthusiasm and integrity make them most in need of its benefits, and most fit to obtain them . . ."[5]

Toward the end of his life, Crowley was unable to communicate coherently. He died a poverty-stricken drug addict in 1947. Despite such an ignominious end, thousands in England and America still follow Crowley's teachings that uninhibited lust and licentious freedom are the way to spiritual truth. As I mentioned in Chapter 6, Ozzy Osbourne wrote a song dedicated to him. Renowned rock guitarist Jimmy Page bought his house, and the Beatles put his face on the cover of their album, *Sergeant Pepper*. Students and critics of occult literature agree almost unanimously that Anton LaVey's *Satanic Bible* draws heavily on the teachings of Crowley. His philosophy of "Do what thou wilt" has also inspired serial killers.

Son of Sam

According to author Maury Terry who wrote *The Ultimate Evil*, David Berkowitz (the Son of Sam) was directly influenced by the teachings of Aleister Crowley. Berkowitz once wrote to a trusted minister that his satanic group followed the philosophy of Crowley and practiced ancient magick.[6] Berkowitz wrote, "They (satanic cults) are secretive and bonded together by a common need and a desire to mete out havoc on society. It was Aleister Crowley who said, 'I want blasphemy, murder, rape, revolution, anything bad.'"[7]

Terry claims the Son of Sam now says that he fabricated the stories about hearing the voice of a neighbor's dog tell him to kill innocent people. Berkowitz says he lied because his cult had records of his family members whom they threatened to kill if he squealed. *The Ultimate Evil* asserts that the original Son of Sam investigators failed to uncover a favorite book of Berkowitz's, *The Anatomy of Witchcraft*. In the book, Berkowitz had highlighted passages regarding Aleister Crowley and Charles Manson.

Many troubled teens also find Crowley's beliefs appealing.

CROWLEYISM AND TEENS

Dean, at nineteen years of age, was a dedicated follower of Crowley's beliefs. He called "TALK-BACK" and declared, "I'm a Crowleyite, a step above a Satanist and several steps above a Christian. I'm a thelemic magician."

"Do you talk with Lucifer himself?" I asked.

"No. But I converse with his minions and all the demons in the infernal hierarchy."

"What kinds of sacrifices do you perform?"

"Just animals," Dean replied. "Humans are worthless unless you aspire to the tenth stage of Crowley's teachings."

"But Crowley's life ended in tragedy," I challenged Dean as I had Curtis. "Doing what he wanted as the whole of the law drove him to insanity, venereal disease, and drugs."

"Yes. He was a heroin addict," Dean admitted. "But I won't end up like that in this life. And when I die I'll go to hell."

"But that represents eternal suffering," I argued.

"Sure. But I've already had plenty of suffering in this life. My dad beat my mother and me. At fourteen, I was kicked out to live on the streets. That's when I turned to the teachings of Crowley because I learned not to need love."

Like so many teenage Satanists, Dean had swallowed the instructions of Crowley as a substitute for dealing with deep personal pain. How sad that Dean chose a hero who exalted evil and failed to achieve personal peace. But there could be no question that, in Dean's words, Aleister Crowley was an "evil genius."

SPIRITUALISM AND THEOSOPHICAL THOUGHT

The development of Aleister Crowley's teachings can be understood in the framework of the evolving occult ideology and theosophical thought that preceded him. In the 1800s, a Russian psychic by the name of Helena Petrovna Blavatsky journeyed to Tibet and claimed to have met disembodied higher spiritual beings whom she called *mahatmas*. Her doctrine regarding communication with the spirit world was codified in her books *Isis Unveiled* and *The Secret Doctrine*. In 1875 she joined with two of her admirers, William Quan Judge and Colonel Henry Steel Olcott, to form the Theosophical Society in New York.[8]

H. P. Blavatsky determined to investigate the unexplained laws of nature and the latent powers of man. Her spiritual cosmology arranged deities under a Lord of the World, who commanded emanating spirits named Master Morya, Master Koot Hoomi, and Jesus.

Current advocates of Crowleyism, like Curtis McQuirt, continue to mix Christianity, the occult, and theosophical thought, as Blavatsky did. Consequently, the ideas of Crowley and other black magicians are presented in a light more acceptable to some Christians.

Eventually the prestigious Society of Psychical Research in Britain investigated Blavatsky's claims and found them wanting. She was accused of being a magician, hypnotist, and charlatan. Helena Petrovna Blavatsky died in disgrace as a lonely, obese, miserably sick woman.

Spiritualism in America

While Blavatsky and others explored mysticism in Europe, Spiritualism in America was also having a heyday. Jackson Davis's book, *A Divine Revelation*, became a standard work for those seeking communication with the dead. Seances were organized to call forth ectoplasm, a foul-smelling, milky-white substance exuding like an umbilical cord from the mouth of a medium. Out of ectoplasm, apparitions were said to appear. Spirit messages, from the profane to the refined, were codified into the Seven Principles and Nine Articles of organized Spiritualism.

The general conclusions of Spiritualism ran counter to prevailing Christian doctrine. To the nineteenth century occultist, Infinite Intelligence was God, original sin was a myth, and the crucifixion of Christ "an illustration of the martyr's spirit." Automatic writing, planchette-talking boards, trance-speaking, and materializations were sought by millions.

Contemporary Satanism in America owes a debt of gratitude to the Fox sisters, Margaretta and Kate of Hydesville, New York. In 1848, their tales of tappings by a departed spirit swept the frontier. News of the phenomenon reached the White House. Abraham Lincoln appeared amused, but his wife, Mary Todd, persuaded Abe to invite professional mediums into the mansion. In vain they attempted to contact the president's late son, Willie, who had died at age eleven.

Others of the era followed suit. Poet Walt Whitman rhapsodized about being part of the eternal cosmic consciousness in "Song of Myself." Across the sea in the British Isles, Irish poet William Butler Yeats belonged to the secret occult society that had attracted Crowley, the Golden Dawn. Yeats attended seances, performed mystical experiments, and once tried to raise the ghost of a dead flower. Sir Arthur Conan Doyle, creator of Sherlock Holmes, was another firm believer in spiritualism.

THE POWER OF MAGICK

All schools of the occult share a common belief in the power of magick (spelled with a "k" by devout adherents of the craft). Magick is not new to mankind and has been the province of shamans, alchemists, and witches for centuries.

Modern groups tend to draw their inspiration from the Jewish Kabbalists of the Middle Ages. Kabbalists believed that sacred writings could be secretly deciphered by understanding the hidden numerical meaning of letters. They traced their heritage to Babylon and to the thirteenth century *Book of Zolar* of the medieval Knights Templar, whose first mission was to protect Jerusalem for Christian pilgrims. Unfortunately, the Templars evolved into a magical society based on gnosticism.

Following the Middle Ages, magical groups were persecuted by the Roman Catholic church as heretical. With the rise of eighteenth century rationalism, formerly esoteric associations began emerging again. The Societas Rosicruciana (Rosicrucians) appeared, and the Kabbalistic writings of Eliphas Levi surfaced. All insisted that ritual magick was the universal world religion, with entities on astral planes the source of undeniable spiritual truth.

The most pervasive secret orders of ritual magick have been the *Ordo Templi Orientis* (OTO) lodges, originally founded at the turn of the twentieth century by Karl Keller, and headed in England by Aleister Crowley. Scientology's founder, L. Ron Hubbard, also reportedly became associated with the *Ordo Templi Orientis*, although today's Church of Scientology disavows any association with the OTO.

Internal organizational structure of the OTO was based on Freemasonry type degrees. To OTO's degrees, Crowley added an eleventh homosexual degree as part of the Temple's ritual sex magick. Keller, a Viennese, toured the Far East and studied the Hindu tantric sex philosophy of yogis. He returned to combine them with Masonic rituals.

At OTO ceremonies, the baphomet symbol of Satan was openly displayed as a source of sexual power. Members believed that when their own sexual energy was aroused during magical ceremonies, they should identify with certain gods and goddesses as the source of their erotic enthusiasm. According to Crowley, the ultimate test of magical adeptness was to achieve intercourse with invisible astral beings, especially demon entities (incubus and succubus).

In America today, secret thelemic occult orders are currently enjoying a resurgence. One group publishes *The Newaeon Newsletter,* whose stated purpose is to "further the Great Work of the Beast 666, Our Father, Aleister Crowley, and to assist in the greater establishment of Thelema, whose Word is ABRACADABRA, and whose Law is Love."

Christians are warned by Thelemites, "Jesus shall never return for it was never meant to be. But the Christ, the Logos of the Aeon, the New World Teacher hath come already and his name was Aleister Crowley, the Beast 666!"[9] Other magical groups drawing on the traditions of Crowley and his followers include the Ancient and Mystical Order of the Rosae Crucis (AMORC—Rosicrucians), the New England Institute of Metaphysical Studies, and the Ordo Templi Astarte.

Teenagers often phone to "TALK-BACK" with a philosophy that represents the confusion of theosophical thought, spiritualism, and magick. A caller named Jason followed the magick tradition that Jesus was a medium and Lucifer His equal. "It's the Christian god who robs and steals," Jason said. "Christianity is a two-thousand-year-old myth."

"How do you know that?" I asked.

"The spirits tell me. I've been communicating with them since I was three. They were passed on to me by my ancestors."

"How deeply have you been involved with magick?"

"I was a satanic high priest for a while," Jason admitted. "I appreciate the work Crowley did with the Golden Dawn."

I would not let Jason laud Crowley without reminding him, as I do all callers who exalt Crowley's deviant behavior, that Crowley was a homosexual, a sadist, and a murderer.

"Do you have a demon?" I asked, wanting to know more about Jason's interest in spirits.

"Yes. But I got rid of it by telling it to leave. It's part of the power that's yin and yang, negative and positive. All I have to do to make evil leave is call on the positive. I'm the one in control."

Like Jason, students of magick believe that occult arts allow them to be in control of their destiny by manipulating reality. Specific deities and spirits, considered to be either literal or archetypal, are invoked. The ceremony is often elaborate, involving special clothing, chanting, meditation, and sacred objects. The devotee may assume the name of a spirit being or a past expert. Distinctions are made between "invocation," calling down cosmic forces, and "evocation," calling forth forces from the depth of the self.

Magick is not an evangelizing belief system, since only an elite few are believed to be capable of understanding its esoteric mysteries. Most are either born into it or lured to it by serious study of the occult. But almost all adherents have one thing in common. Their attraction to magical mysticism results from unresolved personal problems.

"How did you end up in magick and Crowleyism?" I asked Jason.

"I started using drugs at the age of six," he answered. "A family member I trusted gave me some pot. By the age of fourteen I was hooked on heroin."

"Who in your family gave you the drugs?"

"It doesn't matter!" he responded angrily.

What Jason wouldn't admit over the air, he did acknowledge to a phone counselor. Drugs weren't the only problem that a family member had put upon him. Someone he loved and trusted had sexually molested him.

"Are you too proud to admit that the occult magick you're doing is evil, and you need to ask God's forgiveness?" I asked Jason.

"Not too proud," he answered. "Too hurt."

"Have you ever thought about giving your life to God?" I inquired.

"I did once. But now I've blasphemed God and committed the unpardonable sin."

"No, you haven't," I assured him. "If you had, you wouldn't care enough to call me and discuss spiritual things."

"I'm still not going to worship your stupid God," Jason retorted. "Besides, it isn't God who's the problem. It's the people."

Unfortunately, our conversation ended there. Jason was unwilling to reconsider the dangers of summoning spirits and adhering to the philosophy of Aleister Crowley. But Jason did make an important point.

After years of talking with teens involved in Satanism, Crowleyism, and magick, one consistent theme recurs. Jason hit it on the head. It isn't God that teenage Satanists are rejecting. It's the people of God they're angry with.

It's easy to blame the creeds of Crowleyism for spiritually derailing a generation. Unfortunately, too many young people have gotten off track because we didn't love them as we should have.

12

That Old Black Magic

She became a sorceress at sixteen. Her black cloak, dark eye makeup, and the magic wand she carries make her look the part more than most modern witches. Laurie Cabot has been christened the official witch of Salem, Massachusetts. She constantly crusades for her religion, as when I debated her on the "Oprah Winfrey Show." But Laurie Cabot is a media-manipulated caricature of the authentic article.

On "TALK-BACK with Bob Larson" we get calls from real witches like Cracinda, Salina, and Jay, who are typical of those desperately seeking a way out of witchcraft.

Cracinda

Cracinda was a third-generation witch whose aim in life was to destroy Christians. Unlike many teenage witches who get the idea of witchcraft from a tabloid ad or a pulp paperback, Cracinda had been raised to follow the craft. As a child she was reminded that her ancestors for generations had been witches.

"I have an eleven-year-old niece who has tried to kill herself," she explained. "I decided that I needed to change masters if I'm going to be able to help her."

In the midst of the conversation, Cracinda's coven high priest walked into the room. Still, courageously and very quietly, Cracinda affirmed her desire to leave the world of witchcraft behind.

"I was forced to sacrifice my first-born daughter to Satan when

160

she was six months old," Cracinda admitted. "Now I have a nine-year-old son, and I don't want him to follow in my footsteps."

Salina

Salina was a witch high priestess who had participated in animal and human sacrifice. "I'm a medium and have been involved in necromancy and demonology. Help me, Bob," she cried out. "Salina isn't my real name. It's a spirit name."

"Have you been through ceremonies in which you've sold your soul?" I wanted to know.

"Yes, by letting my blood. In the palm of my hand I have etched a pentagram with a crescent moon and star," Salina explained. "Please warn your listeners that they can't play games with the devil."

"Do you want out of witchcraft?"

"Yes, but I'm afraid I'd be dead. I've seen and heard too much. They won't let me live."

Jay

Jay was only eighteen, but already he had been brutally introduced to the underworld of black witchcraft.

"I've been an atheist all my life," Jay explained. "But three years ago I joined a coven—I can't reveal its name—just for fun, especially for the drugs they did. Then at my initiation they sacrificed five kittens. I didn't know what I was getting into."

"Is that all they did?"

"No," Jay said. "They made a ring of fire with gasoline and marked a pentagram in the center. They first killed a rabbit and put its blood in a bowl. Then we drank it. They're going to do this ritual again at Halloween."

"What frightens you the most?" I inquired.

"They said something about my killing someone and then having the power of ten thousand souls. I'm afraid if I stop they're going to come and get me."

WICCA, THE OLD RELIGION

Witchcraft is known by several names, including wicca (wise ones), the old religion, womanspirit, goddess worship, or simply the craft.[1] Witches may also be called druids, the Gaelic word for wiseman or sorcerer. The term *witch* is generic, referring to both men and women. Though the word *warlock* generally is applied to male witches, adherents of the craft deny this distinction.

The history of witchcraft dates back to paleolithic times and the worship of the goddess of fertility. She presided over a cult that celebrated the seasonal cycles of nature. More importantly, she provided a spiritual framework outside the patriarchal religions. The evoking of magical powers by wiccans for healing is found in the legends of Mesopotamia, Egypt, and Canaan.

As the children of Israel entered the Promised Land, Jehovah laid down strict injunctions against involvement with such practices.[2] Traditionally, witchcraft fell into two categories, white witchcraft practiced by tribal leaders who supposedly sought the good of the community and sorcery that concerned itself with curses and revenge. In the Old Testament, both were presented as opposing God, and practicing witchcraft was punishable by death.[3] King Saul lost his life for consulting with the witch of Endor.[4]

In Greece and Rome, beneficent sorcery was officially approved. Certain goddesses, such as Diana and Hecate, were associated with malevolent magic and bloody sacrifices that occurred during the darkness of night. Hecate appeared in three forms: as Selene, the moon in heaven; as Artemis, the huntress on Earth; and as Persephone, Queen of the Underworld.

When the Romans conquered England, witchcraft was already practiced there by the druids, who were well-established throughout Britain and Gaul. The druids were knowledgeable in medicine and the use of herbs. Their universal remedies were mistletoe and serpent eggs, since both supposedly attracted astral light.

HISTORICAL RESPONSES TO WITCHCRAFT

Fear of witches was prevalent in medieval Europe, and such deviltry was usually associated with women. Eventually, legal authorities instituted the death penalty for the practice of such superstitions. In the fifteenth century, the church established dogma concerning demonology that linked witches to the devil, especially when they cohabited with him sexually (incubus). During the so-called Burning Times of A.D. 1300–1600, an estimated nine million people were killed because they were accused of witchcraft.

Ever since, witches have been trying to live down that reputation of devilish collaboration. The famous Salem witch trials in America were one of the last public outcries against the craft. In 1692, twenty supposed Salem witches were put to death and 150 were incarcerated. Ironically, this repressive response to witchcraft proved to be one of its biggest boons. Witches could claim they were unjustly persecuted and therefore deserved more rights than they might have been accorded otherwise, a kind of occult affirmative action agenda. Today Margot Adler estimates fifty thousand to one hundred thousand neo-pagans or members of wicca actively practice witchcraft in the United States.[5]

One of Adler's followers called my radio show the day I was interviewing Sean Sellers from his cell on Death Row. The caller introduced herself as B.A.P. (Born-Again Pagan).

"I was in witchcraft deeper than you'll ever be," Sean challenged her. "Where did you get your name?"

"I'm a wiccan and the born-again part refers to reincarnation. I don't do blood sacrifices or anything like that. But I suppose you still think I'm going to hell."

"Jesus said, 'I am the way, the truth, and the life and no man comes to the Father except by me,'" Sean responded.

"That's according to your Bible. I worship the goddess. Can I pray to her for you?"

"Sure," Sean said. "It won't bother me."

"Dear lord goddess," Born-Again Pagan began, "please let Sean Sellers and Bob Larson and all the other bigots understand wicca, and that by opposing witchcraft they are causing confusion. That's it."

"No amen?" Sean asked.

"No. That's a Christian thing," B.A.P. answered.

Her philosophy, she admitted, was taken from Gerald Gardner's branch of witchcraft.

GARDNERIAN WITCHCRAFT

Gerald Gardner, who was born in England in 1884 and died in 1964, did more than any other single individual in modern times to revive the ancient art of witchcraft. Gardner was an occultist his entire life, an initiate of the Ordo Templi Orientis, and a friend of Aleister Crowley, from whom he borrowed certain practices.

Though poorly educated, Gardner studied anthropology on his own and was involved in the excavation of a site where the goddess Astaroth was worshiped. He studied occultism with the daughter of Theosophist Annie Besant and was eventually initiated into witchcraft. The publication of his book *Witchcraft Today* led to a revival of interest in the craft in England.

On the Isle of Man, Gardner operated a witchcraft museum and accepted initiates into training. Each coven was headed by both a high priest and priestess. Membership was limited to couples. Worship occurred in the nude ("skyclad"), and power was raised by dancing, chanting, and meditative techniques. Gardner also incorporated ritual scourging, along with karma, reincarnation, three degrees of advancement, and the ritual known as Drawing Down of the Moon. Gardner revered two principal deities, the god of the forests and the god that lies beyond, known as the great Triple Goddess of fertility and rebirth.

Though witches delight in suggesting their beliefs have been handed down from pre-existing traditions, the truth is most witches follow the Gardnerian legacy, which combines occultism with Eastern mysticism. By calling themselves Gardnerian, modern witches refer to specific covens that claim a chain of apostolic succession from Gardner's own coven. Even witchcraft leaders admit that Gardner had no access to an original coven or pagan tradition. Many of the craft claim that Gardner was sexually obsessed and fraudulently devised a system of occult succession. Alexandrian witches, closely related to the Gardnerians, follow Alex Sanders, a disciple of Gardner who claimed to be the "King of Witches" in England.

Modern Witches in America

Witchcraft in America was revived by Dr. Raymond Buckland, an anthropologist, and his wife, Rosemary, who studied under Gerald Gardner and brought his brand of wicca to America in the 1960s. Witch Sybil Leek, who started with Gardnerian rituals, also came to America in the 1960s and established several covens. The Religious Order of Witchcraft was incorporated in 1972 in New Orleans, Louisiana, by Mary Oenida Toups, its high priestess.

In the early seventies Gavin and Yvonne Frost of New Bern,

North Carolina, opened the Church and School of Wicca, which has become one of the most visible and active witchcraft movements in America. The school has operated as a tax exempt institution since 1972. Gavin and Yvonne pay less attention to traditional witchcraft deities and instead promote the development of psychic powers. Since Frost is of English origin, it's understandable that much of the School's doctrine is devised from the sexual ritualism of British magick traditions. Their basic message is that any suppression of the body's desires is unnatural and unwise. Drinking and sex are said to be morally appropriate and the precursors to a long and healthy life. The Frosts also endorse the Gardnerian concept of astral sex with spirit partners (incubus or succubus).

The Frosts insist their branch of wicca is non-threatening, undergirded by the maxim, "Eight words the Wiccan Rede fulfill. If it harm none, do what you will." The Frosts insist their brand of witchcraft is benevolent because "any evil a witch does comes back threefold."

But when I debated the Frosts on "Larry King Live," they admitted that it is all right to inflict physical harm on an enemy if by doing so a witch may be able to educate that person's soul. They even acknowledged that on the way to the television show they had put a hex on a taxi driver who irritated them.

In addition to the Frosts' Church of Wicca, several other witchcraft groups have gone public. *The Church of the Eternal Source* is an amalgamation of mystery cults centering on the culture and occultism of ancient Egypt. Members have generally been attracted by the archeological significance of Egypt, which led them to some kind of spiritual encounter with Egyptian deities.

The Church of All Worlds is nature-oriented, promoting a symbiotic relationship between humans and earth. Instead of rituals, they promote sacralizing the planet as a form of pantheism.

The *Radical Faerie Movement* consists of gays and lesbians who see a connection between their sexual choices and the old pagan nature religions.[6]

Other American witchcraft groups include the *Church of Pan* (espousing naturalist principles, including nudity), the *Church of the Wyccan Rede* (founded on Celtic traditions), *Circle* (exploring shamanistic and neo-pagan paths), and the *Covenant of the Goddess* (a California group which has secured tax exempt status for witch-craft groups).*

Witchcraft has experienced a rapid growth since the British Parliament repealed all anti-witchcraft laws in 1951. Witches no longer need to sequester themselves, worshiping silently under full moons. Now they can publish books and appear on TV talk shows to disclaim society's accusations that they are wrinkled hags spiriting through the night on broomsticks.

WITCHCRAFT AND RADICAL FEMINISM

Today, so-called Dianic cults (based on the ancient Greek goddess Diana) emphasize the traditional goddess of witchcraft. They believe this feminine principle of worship is a de-Christianized and backdated version of the Virgin Mary.

Margot Adler, a reporter for National Public Radio and author of the witchcraft tome, _Drawing Down the Moon,_ wrote, "In our culture, which has for so long denied and denigrated the feminine as negative . . . women will never understand their own creative strength and divine nature until they embrace the creative feminine, the source of inspiration, the Goddess within . . ."[7]

Feminist witches teach that their highest purpose in life occurs when they _become_ the goddess, incarnated by the feminine deity they invoke. Elaborate rituals have been developed to achieve this state, often accompanied by trances and vocal elocutions from the goddess. Disagreements exist among feminist witches as to whether these utterances are actually messages from an entity or only the evoking of the archetypal goddess from within. In either case, the Great Rite employed to achieve this state is considered to be a divine union of the human and the spiritual. As a result, feminist witches believe they have been endowed with psychic powers.

Though goddess-worshiping feminists do not profess Satanism, I mention them because this is one way teenagers, particularly young girls, are being influenced by witchcraft.

Not long ago, a friend of mine sitting in a California coffee shop overheard a conversation between a young woman in her twenties and a girl of about fifteen, who were sitting in a neighboring booth.

---

*Anyone interested in investigating the names and practices of additional witchcraft covens should consult J. Gordon Melton's _Encyclopedia of American Religions_ (Wilmington, NC:1978).

The woman gave the girl a book about druids and explained, "I knew you'd be interested in it since you enjoyed the Arthurian tales I gave you a couple of months ago. The book will tell you much more about incantations and the use of magic for good."

The woman began telling the teenager about witchcraft, its magic, and its "wisdom."

"Ask your mother if you could have some friends over to watch a video with me," the woman suggested. "In fact, your mother might want to invite her friends over too.

"The video is called 'Behind the Veil,' and shows the evolution of society from the earliest times when women were leaders to current times when men dominate. You'll see how the economy and the lives of the people were much better when women were in control."

My friend, who had read portions of the manuscript for this book, immediately recognized the philosophy of Aleister Crowley, in which he divided history into two eras. The woman was telling the teenager about the matriarchal eon of Isis and the male-dominated eon of Osiris, which coincided with the religious historical period of Judaism and Christianity.

The woman went on to associate male domination with Christianity. "Even Christianity is beginning to recognize the superiority of women," she said. "Look at the ordination of Barbara Harris as an Episcopal bishop. Someday our world will not be divided into the artificial designations of male and female."

She began telling the teenager about androgyny, a unisex concept that sees men and women as individuals with both masculine and feminine traits, rather than distinctively males and females.

"I will probably never see this order come into its own," the woman told the teenage girl, "but you may."

That conversation was a mixture of witchcraft, Christianity, and radical feminism taught to a gullible teenage girl by a proselytizing adult. As the mother of two college-age girls, my friend fears the influence this woman and others like her have on teenagers and college students.

Witchcraft Beliefs and Practices

Many witchcraft groups perform rituals which they say follow long established traditions. They claim the leaders of current covens are descendants from earlier witches. Gone are the mystical miscreants of earlier times. Today's witches assert they are merely the counterreligion of Christianity, and they predate the Jewish faith. Rather than opposing Christianity, they prefer to adopt a position of superiority, saying they have selected an older form of worship.

Wiccan beliefs are rooted in ritualism designed to cultivate psychic powers. Their creeds are conveyed mostly in oral fashion with the assistance of the *Book of Shadows* (rituals hand-copied by each individual witch) and grimoires (books of spells such as *The Greater Key of Solomon*). Witches organize in groups of thirteen people called covens, a term that was first used in 1662. The idea of a coven consisting of thirteen may have originated in prehistoric worship of the Horned God when thirteen was the maximum number of worshipers to dance inside a sacred nine-foot circle. Some believe the number twelve was chosen to imitate Christ's disciples, with the coven leader making the thirteenth member and representing the devil. Each coven is usually autonomous except for those groups that owe their initiation to another witch's assembly. Membership is by invitation, and progress occurs through degrees.

They meet regularly (usually on full moons) at gatherings known as *esbats*. Eight major festivals of the year occur seasonally, known as *sabbats* (the Latin spelling for sabbath was adopted in medieval times). These festivals are: *Samhain* on Halloween, the Celtic new year; *Oimelc* (also called *Candelmas*) on February 2nd, a festival of winter purification and the approach of spring; *Beltane* on May 1st (or April 30th, May Eve), the fertility festival; *Lughnasadh* (also known as *Lammas*) on August 1st, the festival of first fruits; the vernal and autumnal equinoxes; and the winter and summer solstices.

During witchcraft meetings, various paraphernalia are employed, such as an athame (double-edged ceremonial knife used to raise the "cone of power"), chalice, sword, magic wand, crystal bowl with a rose (representing the sexual power of a woman's vagina), and pentacle (disc-shaped talisman). The five points of the star-shaped pentagram represent earth, air, fire, water, and spirit, and are used to cast magical spells. Unlike Satanists, who invert the pentagram to place the two points upward (representing the horns of the goat head image of lucifer), witches rest their pentagram (pentacle) with the two points downward. Black clothes are worn to absorb energy during magical ceremonies.

Though ceremonies differ, a general pattern is found in most groups. A round table in the center of the room serves as an altar. An imaginary circle is made with the athame. The priest or priestess goes to each point of the compass to summon the four guardians symbolic of the four elements. Pan, or some coven deity, is invoked. The cone of psychic power is raised and the participants may dance, sing, or meditate. Some participants may face a magic mirror to receive messages. At the end, the circle is banished and the guardians are dismissed. A pentagram is inscribed in the air, and each person embraces the others with greetings of, "Blessed be."

If any of the paraphernalia I've mentioned above is found in your child's possession, or any of the ceremonial procedures I've described is ever mentioned or found written down, you have cause for immediate alarm.

Witchcraft Gods and Goddesses

Worldwide, witchcraft is on the rise. In Swaziland, the king grants traditional healers the same status as graduate doctors. In Zimbabwe, the minister of health says witch doctors are as effective in healing as medical physicians. Nigeria has passed a law integrating spirit mediums into the state-run national health services.

Estimates regarding the number of witches in America is anybody's guess. Witches can be anybody. They don't have warts on their noses, and they don't spirit through the night on broomsticks. They are ordinary people who secretly practice their occult arts without fanfare. Many believe that man has lost spiritual contact with the cycles of earth and the rhythms of nature. Witches say their craft can heal this schism between man and earth through mystical truths and unleashing gods and goddesses who animate our world.

Mention black magic, evil spells, and devil worship to most witches and they respond with disgust or amusement. They dismiss all talk of Satan and diabolical deeds. Witches resent being lumped together with devil worshipers. For one thing, witches don't believe in a devil. They claim to be an elemental nature worship religion with roots in ancient agrarian cultures, which revered the earth as a mother goddess. Christians argue that the witchcraft deity is Lucifer.

The goat image of Lucifer (also known as a baphomet or goat of Mendes) found in witchcraft and Satanism is taken from a biblical reference. Christ spoke of those who followed him faithfully as sheep and those destined for damnation as goats.[8] Thus medieval black masses featured the worship of a goat, an animal then considered unclean. Satanists invert the pentagram, placing two points upward to represent a goat's horns. The single downward point is the goat's goatee. Though witches revere a goat as their horned god of the hunt and death (the lord of the forests, sometimes known as Pan), they deny the symbol equates to the Christian enemy, Lucifer.

Witches say they pay obeisance to principles of the Lady and the Lord. The Lord is a male deity of animals, death, and the beyond. The Lady is the Triple Goddess mentioned earlier in the discussion of Gardnerian witchcraft, manifesting in three aspects—Maiden, Mother, and Crone. Each aspect of the goddess is symbolized by a phase of the moon: the waxing crescent, the full moon, and the waning crescent.[9]

In spite of claims by witches that they are not Satanists, many of my "TALK-BACK" callers like Cracinda, Salina, and Jay are witches who have sold their souls to Satan. The fact is, the gods worshiped by witches and the ceremonial practices engaged in by wiccans vary from coven to coven. To some witches, the deities are thought forms developed over centuries. To others, they are archetypes. To many, they are actual entities. Self-styled adherents of Satanism often draw no distinction between hardcore devil worship and wiccan ideals, often combining rituals from both in an evil amalgam.

Most witches today side with Freud who believed demons were products of the psyche and that demonic possession is rooted in the subconscious. Today's thoroughly modern witches are more likely to be New Age advocates who seek to evoke the god within. They read Tarot cards, seek altered states of consciousness, pursue holistic healing, and practice hypnotherapy.

Official representatives of witchcraft will tell you that the kinds of things Cracinda, Salina, and Jay were involved with don't go on in respectable covens of the craft. That's probably true. But there are many faces of witchcraft and most are not as benign as Laurie Cabot and the Frosts would have you believe.

Most youthful participants of the occult don't get involved with high profile witchcraft. Instead, they read the books and study the ceremonies of organized witchcraft. Then they invent their own brand of the craft. Usually they combine elements of witchcraft with black magic and self-styled Satanism. The resulting mixture is dangerously combustible.

WHAT'S A PARENT TO DO WITH THE DEVIL?

If your child shows any interest in the occult, don't wait until there is a fire to set off an alarm. At the first sign of smoke, get help quickly. Contact a minister, counselor, or police expert familiar with Satanism. Today many public and private mental health treatment centers recognize the problems of youthful involvement in the occult and have excellent cult treatment programs. Their phone numbers are generally listed in the Yellow Pages.

Your child's fascination with the occult could be a passing phase, but even a casual brush with such supernaturalism could lure him into further investigation. Though all forms of witchcraft and occultism are not equally damaging, all have the same essential belief systems that glorify selfish impulses and favor unhindered eroticism over restraint.

Sean Sellers was introduced to Satanism through witchcraft. The method of his induction contains some valuable lessons for parents and counselors seeking to avert youth from becoming involved in either witchcraft or Satanism. I asked Sean to tell my radio audience this part of his unfortunate pathway to devil worship and murder.

"It all started when a senior girl in my high school named Melissa gave a speech to the student body about witchcraft," Sean explained. "I have no idea why she was allowed to do it. She said she had witnessed a human sacrifice and had a piece of human skin to prove it.

"My girlfriend knew I was getting interested in this stuff so she contacted Melissa. Then Melissa called me. She told me, 'You can do black magic or white magic. But white magic is hypocritical. If you want real power, go with black magic.'"

"What did she suggest as a way to get started?" I asked.

"Melissa told me to get *The Satanic Bible* and some ritual paraphernalia," Sean said. "Then she gave me a crash course in witchcraft and Satanism."

"Was she actively recruiting you?" I wanted to know.

"Yes, I think that was the reason for her speech at the school. She had been involved in witchcraft since the age of nine."

"Did Melissa ever mention being networked with any other witchcraft groups?"

Sean paused for a moment. "I think so, but I can't be sure. She was secretive. She controlled when she'd call me and where we'd meet. It seemed like she was in league with someone higher up, but I never met them."

"Do you know if there is any hierarchical structure in witchcraft?" I asked Sean.

"She was always talking about different levels. She said there were nine and that she was at level six. Melissa explained how I could go to higher levels on my own."

"What did she say about God?"

"She said that Christians were weaklings and she had more power through witchcraft," Sean explained. "I was mad at God because a girlfriend had dumped on me, so I accepted the idea. I even wrote a letter to my friends saying that the strength of one Satanist equals ten Christians."

"Do you still believe that?" I inquired.

"No way!" Sean declared. "Satan is a created being. God is the Creator. The only power Satan has is the power we give him."

"Besides the influence of the witch, Melissa, what contributed most to your getting into devil worship?" I wanted to know.

"Every teenager I know involved in Satanism has had problems with his father. Either their father wasn't there because of a divorce, or their father abused or ignored them. That's the way it was with me."

"Why is the influence of a father so important?"

"Because God is our Father in heaven," Sean explained. "Our human fathers represent to us what our Father in heaven is like. Those who don't have an earthly father who loves them may find it difficult to understand the love of God the Father."

"Was there ever a time after you got deep into witchcraft and Satanism that you could have gotten out?" I asked.

"Yes. At one point I didn't want to be involved any more. Melissa and other Satanists told me there was no way out. But one day I got in trouble at school. The vice principal found my satanic books and called my mom. She came to school and took me home. My mother was so upset I finally realized how much I had hurt her.

"My stepfather told me, 'There were times I had to hold your mother crying because she was at work and couldn't make it home for your birthday. She would go without food so she could buy a present for you.'

"I felt terrible," Sean said. "I went to my bedroom and ripped up all my stuff on Satanism. I decided that I loved my family more than Satanism and wanted out. I went to a prayer group. I went to a priest. I went to everyone I could find, but no one took me seriously. No one had any answers for me.

"I would write poems and my thoughts about life and death. My mother read them, but she never really asked me what they meant.

"My parents began thinking it was no big deal and dropped the issue. That was their big mistake. By the time my parents started to realize that my Satanism was serious, I had followed the devil's instructions to put bullets through both their heads!"

The lessons to be learned from Sean are evident. If your child tells you about witchcraft or mentions that Satanism is being publicly discussed in school without condemnation, take immediate action. Contact the principal. Bring it to the attention of the PTA. Go to the school board if necessary. Don't let advocates of evil use the public schools to proselytize for their religions.

Fathers, you are an earthly example of God in heaven to your child. As Sean said, the way you treat your child is the way your child will probably perceive God. Take time to show interest in your child's activities and pastimes. Don't take for granted your child knows you love him. Say so frequently and fervently.

If your child has any involvement with witchcraft and Satanism, don't brush it off lightly. Satanism is serious business with teenagers today. Avoiding the issue could eventually cost you much heartache and many tears. It cost Sean Sellers' parents their lives.

13

Satanic Folk Religions

"It was the first religion. It's 140,000 years old. I spent five years in Haiti practicing voodoo."

"I've been to Haiti, too," I responded to Gloria. "I've seen voodoo ceremonies, and they're not the benign religious exercises you make them out to be. I've watched people stand in fire, eat glass, push knives through their cheeks, and perform licentious ceremonies. And they claim to do it through the power of the devil."

"Oh, Bob," Gloria responded condescendingly, "what you call the devil, I call the Seven Great Powers. They live in Haiti, Brazil, and Mexico. The people rely on them. How can you say they're demons?"

"Who do you say they are? Mythological concepts?" I asked.

"The spirits of voodoo are reality, that's all."

"According to the Bible, all evil spirits are demons of the devil," I challenged Gloria.

"Well, I've met the spirits and I've never been possessed. And I've seen a lot more than you have."

"I'm not so sure of that," I said. "I've watched a voodoo priest put a follower into a trance and make him eat a live dove, shoving it in his mouth beak first. It's hideous."

"If he wants to eat raw bird meat, that's his business," Gloria retorted. "I've talked to the Seven Spirits of voodoo and they're not evil."

The roots of contemporary Satanism can be traced to indigenous

175

folk religions, some still practiced in Third World countries. Off-shoots of these occult religions are also found in the United States. Teenagers are often influenced by these ideologies, either through family background or because of the media. Movies, television, and sensationalist paperback novels have popularized voodoo, Macumba, Santeria, and other forms of occult ceremonialism.

MARKETING OCCULT FOLK RELIGIONS

Not all devotees of the devil are self-styled occultists. Behind today's faddish fascination with Satanism lies a long history of folk religions that has enthralled the masses for centuries. Satanism in America is just one facet of the many-sided jewel of evil.

In Uganda, rebel troops follow a twenty-eight-year-old priestess known as Mama Alice, who is determined to overthrow the government. Believers in her movement think they can ward off enemy bullets by coating themselves with the oil of a local tree. They think that by lobbing stones under Mama Alice's influence, the rocks will explode magically, as if they are grenades. Alice claims to be under the influence of a holy spirit she calls *lakwena*. Though she speaks only a smattering of English, Alice says her spirit can communicate in seventy-four languages. After some of her troops were wounded in battle, Mama Alice offered to resurrect them from the dead.[1]

In America, we may not follow priestess leaders like Mama Alice, but folk religious beliefs are more pervasive than we realize. Tabloid advertisement headlines offer lucky rabbits' feet with the lure, "I personally guarantee you can be rich and have lots of money, and you can have it right now." Normally sane citizens adopt ridiculous superstitions. Flowers on an airplane are bad luck. Never talk about past accidents in an automobile. And if you must be admitted to the hospital, do it on a Wednesday.

Other Americans are obsessed with triskaidekaphobia—fear of the number thirteen, which folklore experts say developed from Christian symbolism (Judas, the thirteenth person to arrive at the Last Supper, betrayed Jesus).

Folk superstitions also appear in other developed countries. In Japan, a teenage girl wearing a Band-Aid on her arm hasn't necessarily cut herself. She may suffer a broken heart. Enlisting supernatural powers for the sake of love by using Band-Aids is a recent fad among Japanese schoolgirls. The girl writes the name of her heartthrob on the inside of her left arm and covers it with a Band-Aid for three days. Within a week, her wish to win over the boyfriend should be granted. Another Japanese superstition involves writing the name of a love object on a pencil eraser. If that fails, Japanese women draw a small white star on the nail of their left pinkie.[2]

Occult supernaturalism encompasses the three categories of hexes, spells, and magic. Hexes induce evil spells, sometimes through round hex signs with colorful geometric motifs. In much of eastern Pennsylvania, you can find farms with hex signs painted on barns to protect animals from disease and other misfortune. Spoken spells supposedly have magic powers, such as curses that cause harm or misfortune. These spells can be an oath, contract, or treaty directed against oneself or another person. Magic uses charms or spells to acquire power over natural forces and involves rituals or incantations.

When slave traders transported West African slaves to the Americas, they also uprooted a highly developed form of indigenous occultism. The African's world was inhabited by a pantheon of beneficient and malevolent deities, which were appeased and cajoled through elaborate ceremonies. To them, religion and magic were integral parts of daily life, not casual considerations. When doubt, fear, or decisions were pending, West Africans looked to their gods for direction.

In the New World, slave masters who feared unifying forces among their subjects banished black magic and hereditary folk religions. To continue their forbidden relationship to the spirits, slaves developed a complex web of secret ceremonies, which they practiced clandestinely in the dark of night. Their objects of devotion were usually animistic spirits of nature, although they also revered their ancestors and continued to communicate with family members after their deaths.

BLACK MAGIC

Black magic, the ancestor of today's Satanism, is the most violent and cruel of all pagan practices. It believes each person's desires for sex, revenge, anger, and power must be ritualized and released. Black magicians admit that some of the spirits they consort with are "lords of darkness" and must be approached cautiously. Once wrongly summoned, such an entity can be dangerous. Occult lore abounds with tales of alchemists and spiritists who conducted rituals improperly and invoked dark forces that drove the summoner to suicide or insanity.

Black magicians claim there are several means of protection against such pernicious forces. One is constructing a magic circle of security before you arouse discarnate beings. Fetishes and charms are also employed to ward off evil. Anthropologists who have studied endemic ceremonial magic in primitive cultures say that curses and spells can work if the persons to whom they are directed believe in their power. Followers of the black arts are always trying to counter the malicious intent of their enemies.

WESTERNIZED FOLK RELIGIONS

Voodoo, which was brought to the West Indies by African slaves, is the best-known and most widely-practiced black art in the Western hemisphere. Though usually associated with Haiti, it also thrives in America. In Florida, a third-grade student received official approval to skip school so she could participate in a ceremony to become a voodoo priestess.[3] In Vicksburg, Mississippi, a pharmacist's drugstore offers potions to drive away evil spirits, lawsuits, and unrequited lovers.[4]

In Fairfield, Connecticut, police investigated the death of a baby whose body was disfigured and surrounded by black magic amulets.[5] In Beaufort County, South Carolina, a group of Harlem blacks has established the Yoruba Village of Oyo Tunji for practicing voodoo. Headed by Oyo Tunji, who traveled to Haiti and was initiated into voodoo in Cuba, the village contains temples dedicated to various deities.[6] In fact, there are more hardcore adherents of voodoo in New Orleans, Louisiana, than in Haiti!

VOODOO

Voodoo (known to anthropologists as *vodoun*, from the Dahomey West African word for protective spirit) is more than a folk religion. It has played a powerful role in Haitian politics. The infamous Haitian slave revolt of 1791, led by Henri Christophe, began at a voodoo ceremony on a hot August night. In exchange for freedom from the French, participants pledged the ongoing allegiance of their nation to Satan. Observers of Haitian politics wonder if there might be some veracity to the pact.

For years, Francois Duvalier, "Papa Doc," held dictatorial sway by intimidating the populace with his legendary voodoo powers. The common people believed he was the incarnation of Baron Samedi, the voodoo god of death. Duvalier named his security force after the legendary Haitian bogeymen who snatched way naughty children: Tontons Macoutes. To frighten enemies, Papa Doc kept the skull of a rival at his desk.

After Duvalier's death in 1971, Jean-Claude, "Baby Doc," took over. He changed the colors of the Haitian flag to red and black, the colors of voodoo secret societies. When "Baby Doc's" regime began to unravel, he called on voodoo priests to help him control the unrest.

Zombieism

The book and movie, "The Serpent and the Rainbow," which was based on the story of Clairvius Narcisse, alerted millions of Americans to the realities of voodoo. Narcisse was pronounced dead at the Albert Schweitzer Hospital in Haiti in 1962. Yet in 1980, a man claiming to be the deceased Narcisse introduced himself to the dead man's sister, Angelina Narcisse. She had been at her brother's deathbed eighteen years earlier. Angelina screamed in horror when the man used a childhood nickname only close family members knew and no one had used since her brother's death. The man said that his brother had attempted to kill him over a land dispute, and that a voodoo sorcerer turned him into a zombie after extracting him from his coffin. "The Serpent and the Rainbow" suggested that a powerful potion was the source of Narcisse's temporary trance.

Zombieism is the most extreme practice associated with voodoo. The state is induced by a powerful potion, which contains ingredients from a species of puffer fish and a specific toad. The chemicals contain hallucinogens, anesthetics, and other psychoactive substances that affect the heart and nervous system. Witch doctors say a zombie must be exhumed within eight hours or the body will die of asphyxiation. The zombie is exploited as a slave after retrieval from his state of intoxication.

Voodoo Practices and Rites

Voodoo priestesses *(mambos)* and priests *(hougans)* prepare *gris-gris* (pronounced gree-gree) bags for attracting love and prosperity. Voodoo dolls do exist, but are not commonly used as fetishes. Most voodoo priests do not admit to practicing black magic, although they say all hougans must first learn black magic to fully understand white magic. As a voodoo priest in Haiti explained to me, "To untie a knot, you must first know how it is tied."

Each voodoo believer is assigned a spirit at birth, his own guardian god who supposedly protects and guides him. The spirit's identity is revealed through an initiation ritual performed by a voodoo priest. The ongoing relationship with the god is intensely personal. A good life is ensured if the god is treated well. Most adherents set aside a part of their house for a small altar with a statue of their god. They constantly appease their spirit by placing his favorite food and drink on this altar.

The purpose of a voodoo rite is to summon the *loa,* or voodoo spirits, which then possess one or more of the congregants. Loa may be gentle if the *rada* rite is used, or bloody if the *petro* ceremony is employed. A Grand Master spirit, known as Damballah, is said to preside over all loa. Pentagrams are considered appropriate symbols for women and the Star of David for men.

One evening in Port au Prince, Haiti, I had the opportunity to witness an authentic voodoo ceremony. A full moon shone upon a calm, sultry night. When I arrived, the head voodoo priest invited me to take a front row seat. I waited for more than an hour as a contingent of African-style drummers created an incessant beat. Then the ceremonial participants arrived. They danced erotically and frantically to the rhythms, gradually losing their inhibitions. A male and female dancer simulated acts of sexual intercourse.

One by one, the dancers became possessed as the evening neared its high point. Haitians refer to a voodoo celebrant who is possessed as being "ridden by a horse," literally "mounted" by the god. The person loses motor control and falls into what resembles a cataleptic seizure. Afterward he may perform seemingly paranormal feats.

A large black male, chosen to lead the ritual, stepped into a small fire built in the center. Then he picked up a red hot piece of firewood and put it into his mouth, flames first. He bit off the end of the burning log and slowly chewed the glowing embers without any apparent pain or blistering. Next he took a dozen three-inch-long pins and pierced his cheeks; leaving them there, he resembled a human pin cushion. Finally he took an empty glass and bit off a corner, chewed the glass, and swallowed it. I was no more than six feet away the whole time, taking photographs and carefully monitoring each part of the ritual to watch for trickery. To conclude the ceremony, the other participants danced wildly for at least an hour until the tortured leader fell into a deep trance and was carried away.

The rest of the ceremony was devoted to animal sacrifices and the eating of live doves and chickens. Most interesting was the final appeasement of the voodoo gods. The priest knelt with a bowl of powder. Taking a small amount in his hands, he gradually let the powder sift through his fingers, creating an intricate design on the ground. He saw the puzzled look on my face and explained, "I'm creating a symbol to invoke the goddess of water, Agua." He pointed to the clear sky above him.

Cr-r-rash!

Seconds after the priest finished his ritualistic motif, thunder exploded with a deafening roar and lightning struck a few yards away. Suddenly we were drenched in a torrential downpour.

As I quickly gathered my camera equipment to protect it from the rain, the voodoo priest smiled at me and said, "Don't be surprised. Agua always announces her arrival like that!"

Voodoo Influences Upon Teenagers

Though voodoo is seldom practiced as a religion by teenage Satanists, they do borrow many of its aspects. One often-copied idea is the voodoo belief in sympathetic magic, affecting someone by using a voodoo doll or a part of their body to curse them long-distance. I have talked with teens who wanted to get even with an enemy and acquired a lock of hair, a piece of fingernail, or an article of clothing from their victim to effect a spell.

The voodoo concept of appeasement by blood sacrifice is another important part of teenage Satanism. Many youths who kill dogs and cats for the devil got the idea from reading a book or seeing a movie about voodoo like "Angel Heart" or "The Serpent and the Rainbow," mentioned earlier.

Gloria's Continued Defense of Voodoo

I confronted Gloria, the girl who believed in the Seven Great Powers, about my experience at that voodoo ritual. I asked her, "Who do you think is behind the sexual rites in voodoo ceremonies? I've watched voodoo disciples bark like dogs, simulate copulation, and roll in the mud. They act like monkeys and mimic all kinds of animals. It's dehumanizing and degrading."

"Look, Bob, when they are possessed by a spirit, it's the spirit doing it, not the person. They're mentally blank. They don't even know what's going on."

"How can you be so sure these poor people in voodoo aren't being manipulated by some kind of evil power?"

"Well, I was raised a Christian. Then I went to a voodoo ceremony. The priest came to me, took my hand, and drew me into the center of the ceremony. Then they poured some rum into the fire pit. The flames leaped into the air. A spirit threw me into the fire and flames leaped around my entire upper torso. I didn't feel a thing. This convinced me of the power of voodoo," Gloria said.

"What kind of god would want to risk your safety by throwing you into fire?"

"It was their way of showing me they can protect me from anything."

"What did the spirits of voodoo say about spiritual things?" I asked Gloria.

"They told me there is no such thing as sin. No soul is ever lost. If I make a mistake today, reincarnation says I can come back and do it over again."

"The Bible says we die once and then face the judgment of God," I insisted. "The idea that you can keep coming back to get it right is what the Bible in First Timothy 4:1 calls a 'doctrine of demons.' The voodoo spirits have lied to you, and that tells me they're from the devil.

"I've made my choice," Gloria insisted. "I believe what happened to me during the voodoo ceremony more than the Bible."

SANTERIA

Santeria, an off-shoot of voodoo, originated among black slaves in colonial Spanish territories, especially Cuba. Though they converted to Catholicism, the slaves insisted on retaining their African Yoruba spirits and identified them with Roman Catholic saints. Santeria thrives today in the United States among Cuban-Americans and Puerto Ricans.

One of Santeria's main doctrines teaches that the saint-gods must be appeased with blood sacrifices. So, *santeros* (Santeria priests) regularly slaughter animals, which has not gone unnoticed by police in Miami, Florida, who find goats' heads nailed to trees and bags of entrails strewn in pathways. Santeria shares several gods in common with voodoo, including Ogun, Damballah, and Erzulie. In all, seven deities are worshiped. A more sinister branch of Santeria, Palo Mayombe (associated with the Matamoros, Mexico, murders mentioned in Chapter 7), unabashedly appeals to black magic.

Critics of Santeria are concerned that its influence is spreading to the hinterlands of America, attracting blacks, whites, and Spanish. Headless chickens are turning up in city parks and street corners in New York and Miami. *Botanicas*, Santeria stores, openly dispense cult supplies. A 1982 survey by the Roman Catholic Archdiocese of New York City revealed that thirty thousand people, at least 3 percent of the city's Hispanic population, sacrificed animals, and seventy thousand shopped in botanicas.[7]

In Hialeah, Florida, a Santeria center of worship known as the Church of Lukumi Babalu has officially opened its doors. The santero, the Reverend Ernesto Pichardo, says he will perform animal sacrifices for the church's three hundred members. Hialeah City Council members granted a permit for the building, but they did pass a non-binding resolution to oppose animal sacrifices. More

Santeria churches may be established, since about sixty thousand followers of the cult worship privately in Dade County, Florida.[8]

MACUMBA

In Brazil, voodoo is known as *Macumba* (or its variations, Umbanda and Condomble). In the sixteenth century African slaves were imported by the Portuguese to work the sugar plantations. The slaves brought with them an advanced system of witchcraft. Like Santeria, Macumba melded with the Roman Catholic church, and African deities were christened with Yoruba (West African) names. Today as many as forty million Brazilians mingle Roman Catholicism with spirit cults.[9] Macumba and Umbanda alone claim thirty million.[10] Government census forms include Macumba as a religious affiliation, and there are Umbanda radio stations, hospitals, and newspapers.

One evening in Rio de Janeiro, I attended one of the city's thousands of Macumba churches. This one was a small white-washed building on an obscure, narrow street. No one paid much attention when I entered. Apparently the sight of a curious tourist was nothing new.

I sat down on a rough-hewn wooden pew. In front of the church, an altar was crammed with intermingled statues of various orixa (African) deities and Roman Catholic saints. Devotees, dressed completely in white, venerated an idol of Orlorun, the supreme deity. The head priestess, Mother of Gods, watched over the proceedings, incessantly smoking a cigar. Occasionally she would approach a participant and blow cigar smoke all over him from head to feet.

To the accompaniment of beating drums, the worshipers danced far less frantically than voodoo participants. They swayed in time with the beat, periodically twirling like whirling dervishes. Once in a while the orixa would take control of a devotee to vocalize their message. The worshiper would enter a trance and speak in Portuguese, prophesying a message unknown to me.

At other times, the orixa would seize violent control of their devotees. The possessed follower would thrash about wildly, barking like a dog. Some frantic devotees contorted their bodies as if imitating a monkey, making baboon-like sounds. No one in the building seemed amused or offended at such a degrading display of animalistic behavior.

The ceremony concluded when the Mother of Gods performed a healing ritual. Her followers lined up in front of her and approached one by one. They whispered petitions in her ear, and she responded by enveloping their bodies in more cigar smoke. Eventually the participants seemed to lose enthusiasm from exhaustion.

In Macumba, good and evil are less distinct than in traditional religions. Moral directives are not sought. Instead, practitioners seek a benevolent equilibrium of spiritual harmony. As with voodoo, devout disciples may attempt supernatural feats such as walking on coals, swallowing razors, eating light bulbs, or pushing nails and pins through their cheeks. Candidates for the Condomble priesthood must live in seclusion for six months during their indoctrination. At the time of initiation, the candidates' heads are shaved, their scalps are nicked, and blood from sacrificed animals is poured over their heads.

Satanists borrow rituals from voodoo, Santeria, Macumba, Umbunda, Condomble, and other westernized folk religions. Self-styled Satanists, on the other hand, use elaborate ceremonies, blood-letting sacrifices, psychic powers, and secret initiations inculcated by voodoo cults as a model for their rituals. These satanic folk religions often introduce those already alerted to the occult to darker, more powerful forms of evil.

MIXING OCCULT RELIGIONS AND CHRISTIANITY

Voodoo and its subjects deny any collaboration with Satanism. In fact, they mimic Christianity, which makes occult religions more acceptable to disillusioned Christians. Many who would not totally jettison their Christian religious heritage can merely add metaphysical precepts to the doctrines of Christ. That's what Kirby did.

"I'm a professional Christian psychic," he said when he called my radio program, "and I'm opposed to both Satanism and the occult."

"What do you mean by a 'Christian psychic'?" I wanted to know. To me, the terms were contradictory.

"I am clairvoyant. I do Tarot card readings and consult a crystal ball. I'm also an exorcist."

"What do you exorcise?"

"Demons."

"Wait a minute! You mean to tell me that you use spiritualism and divination, practices the Bible forbids, and you call yourself a Christian?"

"Yes. Jesus is my Savior. I am born again."

"That illogical," I asserted.

"No, it's not," Kirby argued. "Just because I talk with spirit guides doesn't mean I'm a spiritualist. I desecrate witches' ritual grounds because I want nothing to do with the casting of spells."

"Who are your guides?"

"Gretchen and Shalamar. They totally praise Jesus and the Bible. My main guide is the Egyptian god, Isis."

Kirby's fusing of pagan deities and the Christian God is philosophically contradictory. His espousal of biblically condemned practices and his claim of a divine directive to practice necromancy and divination violates Judeo-Christian precepts. Whatever kind of psychic Kirby is, he is not a Christian psychic.

Yet Kirby's approach to spiritual reality is typical of Lucifer's lure, discarding rational religion for a faith that satisfies man's impulsive yearnings. Voodoo and its offshoots are popular because they offer gratification with little more quantification. True religion demands personal sacrifice and the denial of self-indulgence. Satanism's success rests on a proposal that's hard to turn down—the fulfillment of every rapacious desire without commitment or humility.

PROTECTING YOUR CHILD FROM OCCULT FOLK RELIGIONS

Since black magic folk religions generally attract an adult following, your child probably won't become involved in one of these sects. But teenage Satanists borrow from all kinds of occult traditions. Knowing what erroneous folk religions teach and how they are practiced will prepare you to spot other signs of occult interest.

If you live in a major city with large Hispanic, Cuban, or Afro-American populations, or if your family comes from one of these heritages, beware of black magic cults that could entice your child's interest. Please do not construe these remarks as racist. They are only intended to recognize cultural, ethnic connections with indigenous forms of black magic.

Such cautions also apply to Caucasian parents. They should be aware of neo-pagan movements that capitalize upon ancestral links with Scandinavian mythology, Irish and English occultism, and miscellaneous European superstitions. Jewish parents should be concerned with current and past family involvement in cabala (also called kabbala)—an ancient Jewish occult form of mysticism by which rabbis seek to decipher esoteric meanings in Scripture by assigning numerical values to letters and words. If any members of your family have associated with these forms of the occult, it is important to prayerfully renounce the generational links and instruct your children in proper spiritual values.[11]

It's popular to say, "I won't try to influence my child's beliefs. I won't make attendance at church or synagogue a requirement in our home." But the most spiritually precarious thing a parent can do is allow a spiritual vacuum to exist in the family.

The wisdom of Proverbs contains a clear command: "Train up a child in the way he should go and when he is old he will not depart from it."[12] The best protection against Satanism is a solid grounding in Judeo-Christian theology concerning evil. Acquaint your child with Old Testament instructions against idolatry and demonism, particularly such passages as Deuteronomy 18:9–14. Educate your child regarding New Testament condemnations of sorcery, such as Galatians 5:19–21.

Consult your pastor, priest, or rabbi concerning religious education at your child's earliest age. Make sure everyone in your family knows what the Bible says about God, sin, death, and the devil. When your child is confronted with ideas about reincarnation, communication with spirit entities, getting revenge, participating in occult ceremonies, or contacting the devil, he will know these practices are wrong.

Nearly every teenager passes through a stage of questioning matters of faith and religion. Don't be afraid of such inquiries. Handle them honestly and boldly. On "TALK-BACK," teens relate their worst fears and angriest thoughts about God. The conversation isn't always pleasant. They may be mad at God over the death of a friend or loved one. They are often confused by injustices in the world that seem to indicate God doesn't care. "If God loves me, why did He permit my grandmother to die painfully from cancer?" they want to know. "If God is fair, why do so many people starve to death every day?" they ask.

Adolescence is a time of processing contradictory information about life and making sense of it. Questions about God strike at the core of life's meaning. The competent parent will be prepared for the challenge. Don't run from your child's difficult, often brash protests. Meet them head-on by living a spiritually consistent life. Satanism recruits by accusing others of hypocrisy, claiming a teen might as well worship the devil because evil Satanists are more honest than Christians who say one thing and do another.

On "TALK-BACK," teenagers tell me things they'd never say to their parents because I give them candid answers. If I don't know, I say so. If I do, I don't mince words. Their response is often enraged and combative. I know what they're doing. They play the same game with their parents. It's an effort to test my convictions and to see if I'll back down under pressure. But when I don't compromise and simultaneously show genuine concern for their bewilderment, they usually calm down and listen to reason.

When your child debates you, he's actually arguing with God. He wants answers from above, and your position of parental authority is a divine substitute. His perplexing questions about life must be answered forthrightly or he may look elsewhere for explanations. What you tell him about good and evil is the answer he expects from God. Obviously, you must have these issues settled in your own mind before guiding your child. As you've read my conversations with teens, I'm sure you have noticed how often I combat Satan's lies with Scripture verses. Parents must know the truth before they can use it to expose lies.

One of the most effective ways to protect children from the attraction of the occult is to teach them Judeo-Christian principles like the Golden Rule: "And just as you want men to do to you, you also do to them likewise."[13]

Giving to others is a great good, not as Anton LaVey suggests, "a waste of love." Turning the other cheek is better than vengeance. The child who understands these universal religious truths is unlikely to become a target for Satanism's promise of hedonistic fulfillment.

PART FIVE

Everyday Armageddons

14

Dispelling the Darkness

Even he isn't so sure now. Once, Anton LaVey laughed at the idea of the devil. "Satan is just a symbol, nothing more," he was fond of saying as he invoked the Prince of Darkness. "The devil signifies our love of the worldly and our rejection of the pallid, ineffectual image of Christ on the cross."[1]

The halcyon days of the Church of Satan being front-page news are behind him. Today LaVey collects classic cars and subsidizes himself on one-hundred-dollars-an-hour satanic counseling sessions and royalties from *The Satanic Bible*. Still, he relishes the days of yore and reminds anyone who meets him that satanic rock lyrics, satanic movies, even satanic murders are all stepchildren from his Church of Satan. "Let's give me a little credit for having moved society—up or down—but for at least having moved it," he says.[2]

But LaVey wonders if there really is something malignant out there. He remembers putting a curse on actress Jayne Mansfield's lawyer, who soon died in a car accident. LaVey didn't count on Mansfield being with the attorney at the time. She was decapitated in the wreck.

LaVey muses, "Deep down, I have my speculation that maybe there is a force I've tapped into . . . if I came to believe there was some malevolent force, would I want to do it differently? The answer is no. It's too late . . . There'll be no deathbed confession."[3]

The Roman Catholic church has dealt with the devil for centuries and harbors none of LaVey's doubts. Their Rituale Romanum, codified in 1619, confronts evil as a personal reality: "I exorcise thee, most vile spirit . . . O Satan, enemy of the faith, foe to the human race, producer of death, thief of life, destroyer of justice, root of evil, kindler of vices, seducer of men, betrayer of nations . . ."

THE ATTRACTION OF EVIL

Who are those deceived by the devil? By what means are they enticed? Why do they exchange truth for lies and beauty for ugliness?

Narcissism is the soul of Satanism. The selfish satisfaction of vengeance and of carnal delights are prerequisites for sorcery. Hatred, lust, and avarice are unsavory companions that repudiate God and all that is noble. The teenager who begins to experiment with Satanism doesn't think about hardening his heart against goodness. He seeks only to relieve psychic pain. What results is a barrenness of the soul. At first, it is merely a little darkness intruding upon the light. If a youth continues, like so many you have read about in this book, the curtains of the soul will be drawn so tightly that little light penetrates.

If not reached in time, a teenager interested in the occult embraces evil and becomes dehumanized. I have yet to meet a teenage Satanist who empathizes with others or rejoices in another's good fortune. Barring themselves, Satanists believe the world is comprised of bumbling idiots. They develop the attitude that "we" are the elite, "they" the chumps.

Satanists feel no gladness in the pulse of life. The heartbeat of hell deadens their capacity to be touched by human compassion. It all starts with a decision, a choice to turn from good and invite evil, trading decency for impropriety. They give up on goodness and seek instant gratification. Power over their lives and the lives of others is all that matters.

Although even Satanists want to be loved, they believe love is unattainable; and so they opt for evil. In their lives, love has been capricious. To the Satanist, hate is dependable and predictable. It's always there, and you know the effect of its application.

We must restore to our society the idea that virtue is desirable, that terror does not reign. Love really does conquer all. In spite of the deluge of evil upon us, we must reeducate an entire generation to see that godly meekness has the power to heal. Youth must learn that loving and forgiving beget a hopeful people with a heartening future.

Texas State Attorney General Jim Mattox, who headed up the investigation of the satanic slaughters of Matamoros, Mexico (see Chapter 7), fervently told "TALK-BACK" listeners that the crimes of the drug-smuggling devil cult ironically displayed the triumph of good over evil.

"We cracked open the case because the parents of Mark Kilroy wouldn't give up hope of finding their son," Mattox declared. "The strength of their Christian faith sustained them and even allowed them to forgive the cruel killers of their child. In the end, good prevailed because of love. But good will only continue to prevail if we as Christians worship a living God among us."

Attorney Mattox was bold with his testimony of faith, as he implored my audience, "The lesson of these terrible satanic crimes is that we must care for the least of those in our midst. We must not go about our daily business and forget that we need to love those around us in our families and society."

"You've seen the butchered bodies and smelled the stench of death where human sacrifices were committed," I said. "What can we as citizens do to make sure that the Matamoros massacre doesn't happen again?"

Mr. Mattox paused deliberately, with the calmness of an experienced lawyer trying his case, and replied, "The devil is alive and well on earth. I hope that what happened near Brownsville, Texas, reminds all of us that we need to have a deeper personal faith in God as the only strength to sustain us during times of terrible evil."

Detective Larry Jones, the police officer specializing in occult crimes (see Chapter 7), also believes that spiritual faith is the only antidote to evil. "I would be reluctant to personally get involved in investigating satanic ritualism without knowing I have a higher authority than my badge," he told me. "I know that as a Christian I have access to a more powerful force than Satan."

Detective Jones wants casualties of occult crime to understand that faith can conquer their fears. He says that coming forward to admit what happened is the best way to conquer evil. "As long as victims of Satanism say nothing, these cults can continue. But when the abused no longer remain silent, satanic crimes are exposed. Then the cults don't dare retaliate because it would prove what the victims are saying is true."

LOVE VS. HATE

Attorney General Mattox and Detective Jones are right. Evil will always triumph so long as good men do nothing. Fear will always thrive where the light of human compassion is extinguished by greed and unconcern. I've witnessed the mercy of committed people reaching out with love to one bound by the devil and heard the scream of terror from the discarnate speaking through his victim, saying, "Leave us alone! We can't stand the love in this room."

That wail of despair is the fearful scream of Satan. Our nation and our families must leave no room for evil to abide because we have filled the vacuum of national and domestic despair with the power of redeeming, forgiving love. That task cannot be ignored, as daily headlines testify. Satanic murders in Brownsville, a detonated pipe bomb in an Indiana K-Mart, gunfire on a California playground all affirm a world gone mad. Evil's onslaught is so outrageous that officials at a Long Beach school have built a $160,000 three hundred foot long wall to keep junior high students from being hit by bullets fired from a nearby housing project.[4]

History affirms that evil does not always have its way. The inhumanity of slavery ended. The civil rights of the disenfranchised received protection. The indignity of exploitive child labor was abolished. The suffrage of women was extended. But much more must be done to make evil bow before compassion. Incest victims, battered spouses, abused children, neglected elderly, the homeless and the heartbroken in our midst cry for justice. To turn away from their plight is to bid evil have its way.

The teenagers in our trust must know that ethics are honorable and values are priceless. They've seen enough of looking out for number one. We must give them bold examples of selflessness and sacrifice. Television commercials won't do it. Hollywood horror movies won't do it. Wall Street won't do it. Washington won't do it.

We must do it by example and action, especially if we are parents.

As you read earlier in the book, Sean Sellers is an instrument of grace telling others about the power of love over hate. If he can reach out from his small, confining prison cubicle, you and I can surely carry the message of mercy to those around us. We must give America's youth a reason for their tomorrows and an answer for their yesterdays. The choice before us is the seduction of America's youth by Satanism, or the liberation of America's youth by Love.

Appendices

APPENDIX A

A Parent's Guide to Occult Games

KABBALA: Based on the mystical interpretation of Scripture according to occult rabbis, Kabbala (taken from the word *Cabala*) develops the concept that the unknown of the universe can be discerned by divination. Today's Kabbala game situates a hemispheric ball underneath the center of the game board, allowing the board to tip in any direction. A "magic eye" rests on a spindle in the center. Players are told to meditate and release their psychic abilities.

Much like the Ouija board, Kabbala is inscribed with letters of the alphabet, plus the signs of the zodiac. Miniature Tarot cards are also employed. A marble rests in a ridge around the circumference and rolls in any direction, depending on how the board is tipped. Players lightly touch the Kabbala board, ask it a question, and wait for it to tilt, sending the marble like a Wheel of Fortune apparatus on its way to consecutively select a letter, zodiac sign, and Tarot card to compile the answer. Kabbala is an introduction to classic occultism.

PREDICTION ROD: Based on the principle of dowsing, this Parker Brothers' game asks players to grasp a curved handle from which is suspended a balanced rod with a point at one end. Then players shuffle a set of cards inscribed with zodiac signs and place them in an arc on the board. The Prediction Rod is moved slowly from one end of the board to the other and gradually lowered. If all goes according to the game's plan, the point will be psychically drawn to a particular card for answers to life's problems of travel, romance, and vocation. Fatalism, planetary attraction, astrology, and numerology are all part of the divinatory implications of this psychic primer.

POWERS & PERILS: In this fantasy role-playing game manufactured by The Avalon Hill Game Company, players employ four rule books, one scenario book, and their imaginations to move through the adventure. Playing time of the game, recommended for children ages twelve and older, is unlimited. Five to seven players seek to survive the game and improve their character's strength, stamina, dexterity, and intelligence by eliminating enemies and demolishing monsters. Among the creatures a character can encounter are heliophobic demons (who appear as darkly robed figures), Griffins (winged lions who rape mares), and unicorns (which only nude virgins may approach).

Throughout the game, players cast spells and slaughter each other. A blood vengeance spell dedicates one person to killing another, and a chaining curse creates magical bonds to immobilize the limbs of the affected person. Players cast insanity afflictions on each other to convince vexed victims that the world is out to destroy them. A demon-summoning, accompanied by an offering of the victim's saliva, dedicates the soul of that quarry to the demon or devils summoned. Other characters use spells to help them walk on water or kill grotesque creatures. Drugs are employed as a weapon against enemies and to comfort one's own pain. Bindweed is used both as a paralytic poison and pain reliever. Belladonna induces hallucinations to aid in seeing the future. Quartz and other rocks are also used as a source of power. Crystals protect wearers from disease and corruption and also aid in divination.

STORMBRINGER: This fantasy role-playing game, manufactured by Games Workshop, combines mythology, science fiction, and military science in a grueling escapade through the land of Melnibone. The adventure is based on the works of British writer

Michael Moorcock, creator of Elric, the slaughtering sorcerer hero of a medieval fantasy world called Young Kingdoms. The title of the game is derived from the name of the demon embodied in Elric's black sword, Stormbringer, who drinks the souls of those Elric slays. When Elric is injured in exploits, Stormbringer supplies the life force of the souls he has stolen, and the hero is rejuvenated. Eventually, Stormbringer slays his master and drinks his soul while proclaiming his ultimate evilness.

Stormbringer outlines characters two or more players can enact, but details can be reinvented by participants. Players can become hero Elric or any of sixteen sorcery characters. Players roll multi-sided dice to determine character attributes of strength, size, power, intelligence, and charisma, as well as ascertain the outcome of combat and random events. The game implies that ruthless slaughter is acceptable and warns the Game Master that real life friction may erupt between players. Human sacrifice serves as a life force for the deities, and characters may offer themselves or others as a form of worship. Demons will grant wishes if given the sacrifice of a virgin. A graphic picture illustrates a cloaked character standing over a woman lying on a sacrificial altar. Poised with a dagger in one hand and his other fist clenched, he stands ready to slaughter the virgin. The hero of the adventure is the most powerful sorcerer in the land, and his sword slays and drinks the souls of victims.

UNIVERSE TELL ME: Developed by a self-proclaimed psychic, Universe Tell Me operates on the idea that a pointer on a board can be moved by the "subconscious mind," like a planchette on a Ouija board. Two or more people place two fingers on a "shuttle," which quickly moves around a two-foot diameter circular board lined at the edges with Tarot cards. Relevant cards chosen in answer to the questions players pose are bumped from the circle by the shuttle as it psychically shuffles around the perimeter of the board.

In addition to the twenty-two cards of the Tarot's "Major Arcana," "yes" and "no" cards are also utilized, as with the Ouija board. Game promoters say that psychokinetic energy (mind power) manipulates the shuttle. Minute musculoskeletal movements unconsciously triggered by thoughts are one possible explanation. Those who believe in occult supernatural forces must wonder whether Universe Tell Me is a clever device for making players vulnerable to alien input from evil, transcendental sources.

WARHAMMER: Designed for two to six players, Warhammer is a fantasy role-playing game guided by a Game Master who plans the adventure, sets traps, and gives characters skill tests. Game figures may be used but imaginations are usually preferred. Players roll dice to determine the characteristics of players. They may choose a career such as grave robber, thief, druid, or troll-slayer. Among the skills characters use are bribery, torture, divination, and spell casting. Players can even cast diseases or disorders like tomb rat disease, alcoholism, anorexia, or schizophrenia on each other.

Characters assume contact with the dead, and may use a summoning spell to cause corpses to burst through the ground to serve the necromancer. Demons can be summoned with or without the use of a pentagram. Characters evoke gods ranging from Morr, the god of death and controller of all dead souls, to Khaine, the lord of murder and patron of assassins and murderers, who periodically receives human sacrifices. Players slaughter monsters and each other with spears, knives, and bombs.

WARLOCK OF FIRETOP MOUNTAIN: Adventurers must move their characters from an Entrance Area to the Warlock's Treasure Chest using skills and principles similar to other fantasy role-playing games like Dungeons & Dragons (D&D). A character is chosen by rolling dice, which provides components for skill and stamina. Like D&D, characters possess supernormal powers and are armed with mystical powers. Evil monsters to be encountered are The Undead, Hexmaster, and Hellbound. Treasure Cards players hope to attain are Poison, Potion of Strength, Magic Sword, and Hypnotic Eye. Characters are encouraged to slaughter and plunder in their quest to become the sole possessor of the Warlock's treasure. If an adventurer dies at the hand of another player, the victor can claim the dead person's provisions. Consequently, it is advantageous to kill the characters of other players. Success is secured with the help of luck and cards permitting death and destruction.

APPENDIX B

A Supplemental Guide to Dungeons & Dragons®

Concern about Dungeons & Dragons (D&D) compelled me to devote an entire "TALK-BACK" program to the subject. My guest was Dr. Thomas Radecki, research director of the National Coalition on Television Violence. A practicing psychiatrist and college professor, Radecki provided my audience with a psychological evaluation of D&D and other fantasy role-playing games.

Dr. Radecki has documented 123 cases of homicides and suicides for which he blames D&D. He has testified as an expert witness in eight murder trials in which D&D was criminally implicated.

Radecki claimed brutal murders, rapes, and crimes have been patterned after characters D&D players concoct in the game. He cited one example in which a nineteen-year-old Utah boy choked, raped, and sadistically disposed of a fourteen-year-old girl. Radecki surmised that the murderer/rapist, who slaughtered evil female D&D characters to survive in the game, was unable to distinguish fantasy from reality when he committed the heinous crime.

I told Dr. Radecki that many of my callers argue that D&D players who violate and slay people in real life are mentally unbalanced. Radecki responded that, although some D&D players are emotionally troubled from the start, most are honor students with brilliant futures. Radecki pointed out that role-playing is a powerful teaching tool of both positive and negative behavior. Unfortunately, fantasy role-playing games like D&D encourage evil. They reward players with power points for casting curses and remorselessly slaughtering each other.

I questioned Dr. Radecki about Gary Gygax, inventor of Dungeons & Dragons, who has protested that his creation is only a game. Radecki responded that in D&D manuals, Gygax encourages players to become their characters and even uses Adolph Hitler as a role model of charisma. Furthermore, Radecki pointed out that the game discriminates against women by portraying them as erotic objects of lust and aggression.

Radecki warned that many players lose the ability to distinguish between fiction and fact. He says children who play the game may be desensitized to violence in varying degrees and suggests they get help from a minister or counselor. Radecki advises parents and grandparents to gently, but firmly, steer youngsters away from D&D and similar fantasy role-playing games.

APPENDIX C

A Parent's Guide to Black Metal Music

ANTHRAX: Anthrax named itself after a deadly disease, admitting they don't like things that are "safe and pretty." Youngsters yearning for profanity listen to songs like "I'm the Man." During concerts, lead singer Joey Belladonna shouts obscenities to the audience, who scream them back. On their album, *State of Euphoria*, Anthrax guffaws at God and televangelists in "Make Me Laugh." Anthrax also seems to metaphorically mandate vengeful murder in a spiteful song called "Misery Loves Company," which ends with the line, "I'll kill you."

DANZIG: Glenn Danzig, formerly with the Misfits, is a heavy metal hero of the eighties. He collects Japanese monster toys and sings about Satan. The cover of his latest LP, entitled *Danzig*, depicts a goat's skull, the symbol of satanic allegiance. Grisly songs on the album applaud a god of deceit and darkness. The lyrics to "Twist of Cain" relate how Satan fathered Cain, enabling him to commit the first murder. In another song, "Evil Thing," Danzig describes how anger keeps him alive in his private hell as a demon-man. During a recent MTV interview, Glenn Danzig commented that war is acceptable because it represents human nature. Man, he said, should acknowledge his good and evil aspects and not be

203

upset at his failures. Danzig's own ethical dichotomy is apparent in such songs as "Am I Demon," in which he asks, "Am I beast or am I human?"

DIO: Ronnie James Dio claims to have originated the so-called two-fingered satanic salute so popular at rock concerts. His imagery ratifies his claim. The cover of his album *Dream Evil* depicts a child asleep on a bed. Satan peers through a window above her, flashing the satanic salute. From under the bed crawl creepy creatures and slithering snakes. In "All the Fools Sailed Away," he sings, "We are the damned . . . we are caught in the middle of the lion and the lamb . . . we teach you sin." Dio's album *Holy Diver* depicts a helpless, drowning minister, overcome by a horned and cloven-hooved devil.

EXODUS: Their album *Fabulous Disaster*, is named after film character Malcolm McLaren's assessment of the Sex Pistols' Sid Vicious in the movie "Sid and Nancy." Vocalist Steve Souza says *Fabulous Disaster* intends to emphasize rawness and violence, epitomized by songs such as "Bonded by Blood" and "Pleasures of the Flesh." *Fabulous Disaster* includes an ode to a bloody, three-day New Mexico prison riot in 1980. Souza calls "Open Season," a song about a psychopathic stalker who butchers a baby-faced foe, "friendly, violent fun."

Exodus accommodates fans who crave ferocity and a headbanging beat with songs like "The Toxic Waltz." The song advocates slam dance brutality, which Exodus enthusiasts take to heart. Vocalist Steve Souza says one of his most memorable Exodus gigs was in Tampa, Florida, when stage-diving fanaticism left one fan with a broken leg.

The lyrics of Exodus celebrate relentless rage in such songs as "Cajun Hell," which tells the story of murderous slaughter in the South. The embittered Exodus also screeches about prostitutes and politicians in "Corruption." The solution Exodus offers for social disintegration is to pitch people into the slam dance pit and slash each other with "Verbal Razors," the title of another Exodus song.

GRIM REAPER: The album jacket for a Grim Reaper release shows death riding a horse with skulls dangling from the saddle. The harness features a satanic goat's head. Tunes include "See You in Hell," promoted with an ad declaring, "The album you'll sell your soul for."

HELLOWEEN: They spurn authority and recommend rebellion. Their songs inform fans they're stuck in a hopeless age of desperation. Headbanging Helloween's album, "Keeper of the Seven Keys," features a cover depicting a struggle between the hand of life and fingers of death over a ghoulish sea of ghosts. The title track of the album, *Keeper of the Seven Keys, Part II,* describes one man's destruction of the devil through divination and his own god-like power. Helloween depicts the devil accurately as possessing the keys to fear, greed, disease, and death. Helloween also advocates libidinous behavior in a song about a perverted professor named "Dr. Stein," who clones his well-formed assistant and has a hedonistic heyday. Blatant blasphemy marks a song called "Save Us." The lyrics advocate the New Age creed that all forms of life are manifestations of spirit.

IRON MAIDEN: Iron Maiden's favorite subjects to sing about are sorcery and savagery. Their fascination with the occult is evident on albums like *Powerslave,* which delves into Egyptian mysticism and magic. On their album, *Seventh Son of a Seventh Son,* lead singer and lyricist Bruce Dickinson belts out songs about demons and creatures of insanity. The album cover depicts Eddie, the ghoulish Iron Maiden mascot symbolizing death, hovering above a gloomy civilization. In his hand, he holds a ripped-out heart, which is also chained to his rib cage. On the other side of the LP, Eddie writes in a journal by the light of monstrous candles with a crystal ball before him.

Iron Maiden celebrates the number seven, which astrologists credit as the number of the moon, in "Seventh Son of a Seventh Son." In a song called "The Clairvoyant," Dickinson relates a struggle between God and the devil for a telepathic child's soul. The boy falls in love with the devil's daughter and eventually kills himself in the song "Only the Good Die Young." Their first claim to fame was the album, *Number of the Beast,* which featured a song dedicated to the Antichrist.

MEGADETH: In 1983, after being expelled from Metallica for anti-social behavior, Dave Mustaine took command of his own group. The son of a Jehovah's Witness mother, Mustaine vocally attacks Tipper Gore and the Parent's Music Resource Center (P.M.R.C.), an organization Gore founded to censor raunchy rock lyrics. In a song called "Hook in Mouth," Mustaine growls about Gore's actions and accuses her of infringing on his constitutional right to freedom of speech. Anyone who has heard his songs may question what right he has to offend the public. In his remake of the Sex Pistols' song, "Anarchy in the U.K.," Mustaine sings, "I am an anti-Christ, I am an anarchist."

Megadeth cranks out songs about spilling blood and stomping guts with venomous anger. Megadeth's album *So Far, So Good . . . So What!* depicts a shell-studded, combat-clad soldier whose melted face leers menacingly from beneath a crude helmet. Amidst the ruins of a nuclear holocaust, he stands poised with a powerful weapon, ready to blast away all living things. (The name *Megadeth* refers to a hypothetical body count of one million deaths from a nuclear war.)

Though Mustaine and band members claim to inform listeners on important issues and deny allegiance to Satan, their first album was entitled *Killing Is My Business . . . And Business Is Good.* "Black Friday," a song from their album *Peace Sells . . . But Who's Buying,* exalts sadistic slaughter. Lyrics declare, "I lurk in the alleys, wait for the kill. I have no remorse for the blood that I spill."

"The Conjuring," also from that album, seemingly simulates a satanic ceremony. The singer says, "I am the devil's advocate" and concludes "I've got your soul."

On another album, Megadeth muses over the fate of a young witch buried alive by her father in a song called "Mary Jane."

Despite such occult collusion, Mustaine says, "We're aware of the subject we write about—witchcraft, satanic sacrifices and the like—but we're not condoning them."[1]

METAL CHURCH: The Metal Church song "Ton of Bricks" describes someone ripping and kicking until "blood begins to flow." Another tune on the album simply says, "I live to eat your bones."

METALLICA: They play songs about "Creeping Death" as concert fans chant, "Die! Die! Die!" Clad in blue jeans, jeering members of Metallica bellow lyrics lambasting war, drugs, and authority.

James Hetfield, Metallica's lead singer and lyricist, was heavily influenced as a teenager by Black Sabbath. Now his band bewitches a new heavy metal generation of kids for whom Led Zeppelin and Black Sabbath are outdated. Hetfield, the son of strict Christian Scientists, wrote "Dyer's Eve," a dismal song about rage directed at parents. Spiteful lyrics accuse his mother and father of putting him through hell with their parenting.

These harvesters of heavy metal sorrow foster defiance among their growing ranks of raunch-relishing, headbanger listeners. Metallica's popular first LP, not-so-subtly titled *Kill 'Em All*, sold 350,000 copies. Although they profess no interest in Satanism, Metallica explored the works of occult writer H. P. Lovecraft while composing "The Thing That Should Not Be," a song that tells of an immortal, sanity-stealing stalker of the shadows.

Though some Metallica songs border on social commentary ("Master of Puppets," "Disposable Heroes," "Leper Messiah"), most of their tunes celebrate suicide, hatred, and hopelessness. In many Metallica songs, death is the only escape in a world of "blackened" banality. Songs like "Fade to Black" from their *Ride the Lightning* album and "One" from the album *And Justice for All* laud death as a welcome friend in a world of frustration, pain, and failure.

MISCELLANEOUS BANDS

CELTIC FROST: A Celtic Frost member sports a leather bicep armband with an inverted cross. On their album "Emperor's Return," Lucifer is featured with his snake-like body entwined around three nearly-nude women.

SAM HAIN: The group Sam Hain, a name taken from the Luciferian Lord of the Dead, spotlights an album called "Unholy Passion." The leader of the group, which is now defunct, says, "I'm really into skulls and bones and things. We are definitely into the gore scene. If you don't understand or realize what death is, you won't be able to enjoy life."[2]

SATAN: The cover of Satan's album, *Court in the Act*, shows a robed skeletal figure rising out of a misty cloud. A bony hand points to the name Satan. The cover of this group's album, "Suspended Sentence," depicts a victim hung at the hands of a ghoulish specter. One song on this album is called "11th Commandment." Its lyrics declare, "You've got to live with reality, don't hide behind a faith."

SODOM: The band, Sodom, has an album called *Obsessed by Cruelty*. Its jacket portrays a skeletal death figure with claw-like fingers dripping blood.

POSSESSED:: Combat Records' band, Possessed, illustrates the album title *Beyond the Gates* with the "s" from "Gates" stylized into a forked tail.

APPENDIX D

Calendar of Satanism and Witchcraft Ceremonies

The calendar of witchcraft, which Satanism has adopted and modified, recognizes eight major holidays called *sabbats*. These are the annual festivals of the old religion of wicca. In some cases Satanism recognizes a different day from witchcraft, as indicated below.

February 1:   Oimelc—also called Candelmas* (festival of winter purification and the approach of spring)

March 21:   Spring equinox

May 1:   Beltane (fertility festival)

June 21 or 22:   Summer solstice (longest day of the year)

August 1:   Lammas or Lughnasadh (festival of first fruits)

September 23:   Fall equinox

October 31:   Samhain or Halloween (Celtic new year)

December 21 or 22:   Winter solstice (Yule—shortest day of the year)

---

*Satanism holiday

Notes

1. Altar of Sacrifice

1. See 1 Timothy 6:10.

2. Murder for the Devil

1. "Networking to Beat the Devil," *Newsweek*, 5 December 1988, p. 29.

2. Maury Terry, *The Ultimate Evil*, Doubleday & Co., Inc., Garden City, New York, 1987, p. 511.

3. Vincent Bugliosi, *Helter Skelter*, W. W. Norton & Co., Inc., New York, New York, 1974, p. 637.

4. "Night Stalker," *People*, 16 September 1985, p. 44.

5. Pat Milton, "Drugs Changed Life of Teen Charged in Satanic Killing," *Ft. Worth Star-Telegram*, 15 July 1984, n.p.

6. David Breskin, "Kids in the Dark," *Rolling Stone*, 22 November 1984, pp. 30–32.

7. *Ibid.*, p. 34.

8. Jimmy Mack, McLean Cummings, and Paul Lauer, "Satanism," *Veritas Catholic Youth Magazine*, March/April 1989, p. 16.

9. Lisa Levitt Ryckman, "Fallen Angels: Incidences of Teenagers Involved with Occult Increasing Phenomenon," *Denton Record-Chronicle*, 9 March 1988, p. 2C.

3. Occult Enticements

1. "D.C. twilight zone: psychics in demand," *The Denver Post*, 4 December 1988, p. 1D.

2. *Ibid.*, p. 1B.

3. Russell Targ, Ph.D., International Transpersonal Conference, 10 October 1988.

4. *Ibid.*

5. Guy Kelly, "Psychics Not Gurus in Turbans," *Rocky Mountain News*, 20 November 1988, p. 28.

6. David Breskin, "Kids in the Dark," *Rolling Stone*, 22 November 1984, p. 84.

7. *USA Today*, 28 October 1986, p. 1D.

8. *USA Today*, 30 October 1987, p. 10A.

9. *Ibid.*

10. See 1 John 4:4.

11. See Genesis 3:5.

4. Ghoulish Games

1. John Weldon and James Bjornstad, "Fantasy Games People Play," *Contemporary Christian Magazine*, December 1984.

2. Howard Witt, "Teen Suicide, Murders Linked to Fantasy Game," *Dallas Morning News*, 31 January 1985.

3. Gary Gygax, *Official Advanced Dungeons & Dragons Player's Handbook*, TSR Inc., Random House: New York, 1978, p. 40.

4. *Ibid.*, p. 48.

5. James Ward and Rob Kuntz, *Official Advanced Dungeons & Dragons Legends and Lore*, TSR Inc., Random House, United States, 1984, p. 9.

6. *Ibid.*, p. 11.

7. *Ibid.*, p. 23.

8. *Ibid.*, p. 26.

9. "The Assault on Role-Playing Games," Game Manufacturers Association handout, 1 March 1988, p. 1.

10. See Matthew 5:28.

11. 2 Corinthians 10:5.

12. Proverbs 23:7.

13. Deuteronomy 18:10–12.

5. Nightmare on Main Street

1. *Billboard*, 4 October 1986, p. H4.

2. "The Horror of It All," *USA Today*, 29 December 1988, p. 2D.

3. John Larrabee, "Slasher Suspect Found Hanged," *USA Today*, 30 November 1988, p. 3A.

4. "Gross Out Movies Are Big Grossers," *USA Today*, 25 April 1984, p. 2D.

5. *USA Today*, 29 December 1983, p. 5D.

6. "We're Drawn to Gruesome, Gory Stuff," *USA Today*, 5 April 1984, p. 2D.

6. Black Metal Mania

1. *Great Falls Tribune*, 14 February 1988, p. 4B.

2. *Hit Parader*, September 1986, p. 48.

3. *Ibid.*

4. Tim Bennett, "Slayer Denies Responsibility for Assault," *Arkansas Democrat*, 30 May 1987, p. 1B.

5. *Ibid.*

6. Legs McNeil, "Somewhere the Devil Is Laughing," *Spin*, October 1988, p. 38.

7. *Griffith*, vol. 1, no. 5.

8. Hans Grieling, "In Satan's Service," *Hit Parader*, October 1988, p. 65.

9. *Billboard*, 6 July 1985, p. 22.

10. Andy Secher, "Led Zeppelin: The Second Coming?", *Hit Parader,* July 1982, p. 7.

11. Stephen Davis, "The Rise and Fall of Led Zeppelin," *Rolling Stone,* 4 July 1985, p. 34.

12. *Ibid.*

13. *Circus,* 29 February 1984, p. 73.

14. George Joseph Tanber, "Cult-Murder Inquiry Focuses on School," *The Toledo Blade,* 20 February 1986, n.p.

15. *Hit Parader,* February 1985, p. 42.

16. *Hit Parader,* February 1984, p. 14.

17. *US,* 21 May 1984, p. 38.

18. Associated Press, "Parents Beware Black Metal Lyrics," *Denton-Record Chronicle,* 9 March 1988, p. 1C.

19. *Griffith,* vol. 1, no. 5.

7. Satan's Opiate

1. Julia Morris and Steve Marshall, "Cult 'Godfather' hunted," *USA Today,* 13 April 1989, p. 3A.

2. *Ibid.*

3. Ed Kiersh, "The Book of Shadows," *Spin,* August 1988, p. 24.

4. Carl A. Raschke, "Satanism and the Devolution of the 'New Religions,'" *SCP Newsletter,* Fall 1988, pp. 22–29.

5. "1,200 child-abuse deaths cited," *Rocky Mountain News,* 3 March 1989, p. 50.

6. Chris Lutes, *What Teenagers are Saying about Drugs and Alcohol,* Tyndale House, Inc., Wheaton, Illinois, 1988, p. 247.

8. Servants of Satan

1. *Great Falls Tribune,* 14 February 1988, p. 4B.

2. Claire Safran, "The Devil Made Me Do It," *Woman's Day,* 22 November 1988, p. 153.

3. Ed Kiersh, *Spin,* August 1988, p. 24.

4. *Ibid.,* p. 68.

5. *Ibid.,* p. 23.

6. Chris Wood, "Suicide and Satanism," *MacClean's,* 30 March 1987, n.p.

7. Lisa Levitt Ryckman, "Fallen Angels," *Denton Record-Chronicle,* 9 March 1988, p. 1C.

8. Anton Szandor LaVey, *The Satanic Bible,* Avon Books, New York, New York, 1969.

9. Matthew 5:39.

10. Anton Szandor LaVey, *The Satanic Bible,* Avon Books, New York, New York, 1969, p. 33.

11. Proverbs 25:21/Romans 12:20.

12. Anton Szandor LaVey, *The Satanic Bible,* Avon Books, New York, New York, 1969, p. 33.

13. *Ibid.,* p. 30.

14. *Ibid.,* p. 33.

15. *Ibid.,* p. 67.

16. *Ibid.,* p. 88.

17. *Ibid.*, p. 89.

18. *Ibid.*, p. 90.

19. *Ibid.*, p. 156.

20. Anton LaVey, *The Satanic Rituals*, Avon Books, New York, New York, 1972, p. 14.

21. *Ibid.*, p. 17.

22. *Ibid.*, p. 19.

23. *Ibid.*, pp. 57–59.

24. *Ibid.*, p. 25.

25. *Ibid.*, p. 77.

26. *Ibid.*, p. 220.

27. See Proverbs 6:16-19.

28. "Children Who Turn to the Devil," Judith Graffam, *The Press Enterprise*, 12 April 1987, p. C8.

29. Claire Safran, "The Devil Made Me Do It," *Woman's Day*, 22 November 1988, p. 152.

9. Sacrifice of Innocents

1. "Tracking the Cattle Mutilations," *Newsweek*, 21 January 1980, p. 16.

2. Larry Kahner, *Cults That Kill*, Warner Books, 1988, New York, New York, pp. 147–148.

3. Derk Roelofsma, "Battling Satanism a Haunting Task," *Insight*, 1 November 1988, p. 49.

4. Kevin Diaz, "Police Expert Warns of Satanism," *Minneapolis Star Tribune*, 27 September 1987, p. 1B.

5. Derk Roelofsma, "Battling Satanism a Haunting Task," *Insight*, 1 November 1988, p. 48.

6. *Ibid.*, p. 48.

7. Lauren Stratford, "With Tender Love," *Satan's Underground*, Harvest House Publishers, Eugene, Oregon, 1988, p. 146.

8. "Geraldo" telecast of 24 October 1988.

9. *Ibid.*

10. Aleister Crowley, *Magick in Theory and Practice*, Castle Books, New York, New York, n.d., p. 95.

11. Richard Cavendish, *The Black Arts*, G. P. Putnam's Sons, New York, New York, 1967, p. 272.

12. Jimmy Mack, McLean Cummings and Paul Lauer, "Satanism," *Veritas Catholic Youth Magazine*, March/April 1988, p. 17.

13. *Nevada Appeal*, vol. 121, no. 86, 23 August 1985, n.p.

14. *The Denver Post*, 8 August 1988, pp. 1, 8A.

15. "Networking to Beat the Devil," *Newsweek*, 5 December, 1988, p. 29.

16. Kevin Diaz, "Police Expert Warns of Satanism," *Minneapolis Star Tribune*, 27 September 1987, p. 1B.

17. "Networking to Beat the Devil," *Newsweek*, 5 December 1988, p. 29.

18. *The Bakersfield Californian*, September 1986, p. 9.

10. Mephistopheles' Manifesto

1. M. Scott Peck, *People of the Lie*, Simon and Schuster, New York, New York, 1983, p. 204.

2. *Ibid.*, p. 207.

3. See Ezekiel 28:13–15.

4. See Isaiah 14:14.

5. See Job 2:1–6.

6. See Matthew 4:8–9.

7. See Matthew 4:6.

8. See 2 Corinthians 11:14.

9. See 2 Timothy 2:26.

10. See Genesis 3:1–24.

11. See James 1:13–15.

12. See Colossians 2:15.

13. See 1 John 3:8.

14. See Matt Roush, "Meet Horror's Heir Apparent," *USA Today*, 22 August 1986, p. 5D.

15. "King of Horror," *Time*, 6 October 1986, p. 80.

16. Wade Baskin, *Satanism*, Citadel Press, Secaucus, New Jersey, 1972, p. 61.

17. Leslie A. Shepard, Ed., *Encyclopedia of Occult and Parapsychology*, (2nd edition), vol. 2 (H-O), Gale Research Co., Detroit, Michigan, 1984, p. 939.

18. *Necronomicon*, Avon Books, New York, New York, February 1977, p. X.

19. *Ibid.*, p. XXVIII.

20. *Ibid.*, p. LIII.

21. *Ibid.*, p. 69.

22. *Ibid.*, p. 218.

23. Larry Kahner, *Cults That Kill*, Warner Books, New York, New York, 1988, pp. 67–71.

24. Arthur Lyons, *Satan Wants You*, The Mysterious Press, New York, New York, 1988.

25. "The Second Beast of Revelation," *Newsweek*, 16 November 1987, p. 73.

26. Maury Terry, *The Ultimate Evil*, Garden City, New York, 1987, p. 306.

11. Aleister Crowley's Creed

1. See Mark 7:21–23.

2. See Revelation 13:1.

3. *The Book of the Law*, Thelema Publications, Kings Beach, California, no year, p. 9.

4. Arthur Lyons, *Satan Wants You*, The Mysterious Press, New York, New York, 1988, p. 81.

5. John Symonds, "Aleister Crowley," *Man, Myth & Magic*, An Illustrated Encyclopedia of the Supernatural, Marshall Cavendish Corporation, New York, New York, 1970, pp. 559–563.

6. Maury Terry, *The Ultimate Evil*, Garden City, New York, 1987, p. 303.

7. *Ibid.*, p. 310.

8. *Larson's Book of Cults*, Tyndale House Publishers, Inc., Wheaton, Illinois, 1982, and J. Gordon Melton, *The Encyclopedia of American Religions*, McGrath Publishing Company, North Carolina, 1978, vol. 2.

9. *The Newaeon Newsletter*, vol. 1, no. 1, 22 December 1977, p. 1.

12. That Old Black Magic

1. Various portions of this section were compiled with the assistance of J. Gordon Melton's book, *The Encyclopedia of American Religions*, MacGrath Pub-

lishing Company, Wilmington, North Carolina, 1978, vol. 2, pp. 179–186, and *Encyclopedia Britannica,* 1986, 15 edition, vol. 25, "Occultism: Witchcraft," pp. 94–96.

2. See Deuteronomy 18:9–14/Leviticus 19:31.

3. See Exodus 22:18.

4. See 1 Chronicles 10:13.

5. Derk Roelofsma, "Inside the Circle of Witches Modern," *Insight,* 8 June 1987, p. 91.

6. Margot Adler, *Drawing Down the Moon,* (Revised and Expanded Edition) Beacon Press: Boston, Massachusetts, 1986, 1979, pp. 263, 308–310, 344.

7. *Ibid.,* p. ix.

8. Matthew 25:32–33.

9. Margot Adler, *Drawing Down the Moon,* (Revised and Expanded Edition) Boston, Massachusetts, Beacon Press, 1986, 1979, p. 112.

13. Satanic Folk Religions

1. "Goodby, Mama Alice," *Time,* 23 November 1987, p. 38.

2. *USA Today,* 12 March 1987, p. 5D.

3. "Pupil's Absences for Religions Rites Ruled Legitimate," *Rocky Mountain News,* 8 December 1984, n.p.

4. "Mississippi Pharmacist Offers Black Magic to Voodoo Followers," *Drug Topics,* 3 May 1982, p. 56.

5. "New Jersey Cop Probes Possible Cult Link to Connecticut Baby's Death," *The Press,* Atlantic City, New Jersey, 21 March 1986, p. 6.

6. "Old Yoruba Customs Draw New Criticism, *Newsweek,* 7 December 1981, n.p.

7. Gary Langer, "Blood-sacrifice Cults Spreading," *The Seattle Times,* 25 November 1984, p. 14B.

8. Jeanne DeQuine, "Church Practicing Animal Sacrifices Opens Today," *USA Today,* 17 August 1987, p. 3A.

9. Richard N. Ostling, "Building Bridges in Brazil," *Time,* 21 July 1980, p. 43.

10. "Brazil's Bizarre Cults," *Newsweek,* 27 February 1987, p. 39.

11. See Exodus 34:6–7.

12. Proverbs 22:6.

13. Luke 6:31.

14. Dispelling the Darkness

1. Walt Harrington, "The Devil in Anton LaVey," *The Washington Post Magazine,* 23 February 1986, p. 6.

2. *Ibid.,* p. 16.

3. *Ibid.,* p. 17.

4. "Bullet Barrier Built Around California School," *USA Today,* 17 April 1989, p. 1A.

Appendix C. A Parent's Guide to Black Metal Music

1. R. J. Merkel, *Hit Parader,* 4 November 1987, p. 31.

2. *New Times,* vol. 16, p. 9.

Bibliography

Adler, Margot. *Drawing Down the Moon*. Revised. Boston: Beacon Press, 1986.

Baskin, Wade. *Satanism*. Secaucus, NJ: Citadel Press, 1972.

The Book of the Law. Kings Beach, CA: Thelema Publications, 1983.

Bugliosi, Vincent. *Helter Skelter*. New York: W. W. Norton and Co., 1974.

Cavendish, Richard. *The Black Arts*. New York: G. P. Putnam's Sons, 1967.

Crowley, Aleister. *Magic in Theory and Practice*. New York: Castle Books, n.d.

Encyclopedia Britannica. Chicago: University of Chicago Press, 1986.

Gygax, Gary. *Official Advanced Dungeons & Dragons Player's Handbook*. TSR Inc., New York, Random House, 1984.

Kahner, Larry. *Cults That Kill*. New York: Warner Books, 1988.

Larson, Bob. *Larson's Book of Cults*. Wheaton, IL: Tyndale House, 1982.

LaVey, Anton Szandor. *The Satanic Bible*. New York: Avon Books, 1969.

Lyons, Arthur. *Satan Wants You*. New York: The Mysterious Press, 1988.

Melton, J. Gordon. *The Encyclopedia of American Religions*. Wilmington, NC: McGrath, 1978.

Necronomicon. New York: Avon Books, 1977.

Peck, M. Scott. *People of the Lie*. New York: Simon and Schuster, 1983.

Shepard, Leslie A., ed. *Encyclopedia of Occult and Parapsychology*. 2nd ed. Detroit: Gale Research Co., 1984.

Stratford, Lauren. *Satan's Underground*. Eugene, OR: Harvest House, 1988.

Symonds, John. *Man, Myth and Magic: An Illustrated Encyclopedia of the Supernatural*. New York: Marshall Cavendish Corp., 1970.

Terry, Maury. *The Ultimate Evil*. Garden City, NY: Doubleday and Co., 1987.

Ward, James, and Rob Kuntz. *Official Advanced Dungeons & Dragons Legends and Lore*. TSR Inc., Random House, United States 1984.

Index

About the Author

Bob Larson is a forceful voice in a confused world. Through his talk show, "TALK-BACK," eighteen books, award-winning videos, and television guest appearances, Bob informs his audiences and readers about today's critical issues.

"TALK-BACK," a daily radio talk show aired two hours each weekday, is heard by millions live via satellite in approximately 200 cities in the United States, and in Canada, as well as South America, Western Europe, and North Africa.

Bob's books cover current problems, such as the New Age Movement, cults, and the occult. His videos reach a TV generation, teaching them how to deal with today's social pressures.

Bob has made guest appearances on the "Oprah Winfrey Show," the "Larry King Show," "Straight Talk," and the "Morton Downey Show." He has lectured in more than seventy countries and is the author of *Larson's Book of Rock, Straight Answers on the New Age,* and *Larson's Complete Book of Cults.*

If you or someone you know is involved in Satanism and local counseling is unavailable, please contact the following address for referrals:

> "TALK-BACK with Bob Larson"
> Box 36A
> Denver, CO 80236